T0345616

EASY RIDER

Easy Rider

50 Years Looking for America

Steven Bingen

With Alan Dunn

Guilford, Connecticut

An imprint of The Rowman & Littlefield Publishing Group, Inc.
4501 Forbes Blvd., Ste. 200
Lanham, MD 20706
www.rowman.com

Distributed by NATIONAL BOOK NETWORK

British Library Cataloguing in Publication Information available

Library of Congress Cataloging-in-Publication Data available

ISBN 978-1-4930-4643-0 (hardcover)
ISBN 978-1-4930-4644-7 (e-book)

♾™ The paper used in this publication meets the minimum requirements of American National Standard for Information Sciences—Permanence of Paper for Printed Library Materials, ANSI/ NISO Z39.48-1992.

To my family, Zoe and Beth, and my parents—
thanks for coming along for the ride.

CONTENTS

Introduction and Acknowledgments

A hero is someone who understands the responsibility that comes with his freedom.

—Bob Dylan

Confession. I'm not a member of the baby-boomer generation. I'm not a member of the Woodstock generation. I'm not a biker, a hippie, a beatnik, a hipster, a freak, a straight, a sellout, or a dropout.

But I do love *Easy Rider*.

While I love the film, unlike some of the *Easy Rider* fans who tell their stories below, I never dropped out, dropped acid, joined the Hells Angels, started a commune, retraced the movie's locations, or filmed my own sequel.

In fact, to be honest, I originally avoided the movie entirely.

An inadvertent and recurring wellspring of this book has turned out to be—without my planning on it, or realizing I was puncturing that wellspring at the time—getting people from all walks of life to talk about how they were first introduced to *Easy Rider*. My collaborator Alan Dunn and I have interviewed and solicited reminiscences, commentary, and criticism about the movie from fans and filmmakers and authors and bikers, from people who worked on the movie, and from those the movie has been working on ever since.

I've taken the liberty of reproducing these testimonies, largely unedited from what we transcribed, in order to bring the voices of the film's true believers to the table. These voices illustrate better than I ever could how many different types of people were affected by *Easy Rider*, and how their interest in the film subsequently directed their paths in life.

Given that so many people have shared their *Easy Rider* origin stories with us, it now seems a little evasive not to include such a story myself, if only to offer turnaround as fair play to those whom I've impertinently asked, "How did you discover *Easy Rider*?"

Truth is, I like motorcycles. I've even owned a couple of them, but for some reason, unlike many of those mentioned below, I never saw *Easy Rider* in its original release, or on television in any of its hundreds of often-edited broadcast and syndicated and cable and home-video small-screen presentations. But when I was in college in the 1980s, I worked at a repertory movie theater as a projectionist. We ran classics, current films, foreign films, cult movies, and at midnight, even X-rated fare. Often, when we booked a movie I hadn't seen, I'd go and watch it in the audience, even though I would have to run that same film from the projection booth later in the week. Yet, when we screened *Easy Rider*, for some reason I didn't bother to come in for a pre-watch. Perhaps I was worried that the movie would be one long and already-dated head trip, like some other 1960s "classics," or, even worse, that it would be an ersatz imitation of probably better films which were coming out of Europe during that period.

Anyway, my first viewing of *Easy Rider* took place in a projection booth, while loading and threading and projecting the film from two-thousand-foot reels, and keeping those reels in focus and properly lit while monitoring the presentation through a plate-glass partition, separated from those looking into the light like a priest in a confessional booth. So, because I was not part of the audience—I was actually sort of responsible for the audience—I wasn't able to lose myself in the film, like moviegoers do with any good movie. In fact, I could barely hear the sound over the clatter of the projectors. Although it did seem to me, even then, that Dennis Hopper was saying "man" an awful lot. It also seemed to me that every time I looked through the porthole into the light above the audience, there were beautiful shots of hairy guys on awesome-looking motorcycles up there.

Those images of motorcycles roaring along, with seemingly the whole of the United States as a slipstream backdrop, is what I remembered when the movie ended and I walked home. So, at that point, I hadn't really seen, or heard, the movie yet, except in pieces. Even so, I kept thinking about it. Days later, I was still thinking about it. Who were those two hippies? I'd ask myself. Why were they riding across the country? How did they get those cool bikes? And most importantly, who was Steppenwolf?

I didn't know at the time that *Easy Rider* was a film that could not be diminished, even by watching it as I did: seeing it in small pieces, weaving in and out of the narrative, watching intensely for the projectionist marks on the screen in order to accurately change the reels, and then not watching parts of it at all. All of this, come to think of it, was a decent approximation of being stoned, which is how a great many people saw the film for the first time and ended up being as affected by it as I was.

So, yes, I was not the first to fall under the film's spell without really knowing what the film was about. I may, however, have been one of the first to do so while simultaneously inflicting that spell onto others.

Every movie is made up of images. Film itself, of course, is made up of millions of still images projected to simulate motion. Occasionally, one of these images will somehow, probably inadvertently, prove to be memorable, even life-changing to audiences. *Easy Rider* is a film made up of those memorable images.

Go ahead; pick your favorite. It's fun. Peter Fonda throwing away his watch? Any scene with the men at a campfire? Any scene—every scene—on the choppers? (There are a *lot* of those.) Those zombie-like commune dwellers? Any bit involving Jack Nicholson? The freakish 16mm New Orleans cemetery? Or, if you tend toward the dark side, the fiery climax? (Which all by itself probably kept a lot of would-be Jack Kerouacs off the road in the early 1970s.)

My point is, *any* of these could have made any film—at least briefly—memorable. While very few films have more than one such image, *Easy Rider* has countless of these little "pieces of time," as James Stewart has called them, although it's a safe bet Stewart was not thinking of *Easy Rider* when he said this.

But trust me, if you haven't yet watched *Easy Rider* straight, or outside of a projection booth, you're cheating both the film and yourself. When I finally saw the movie a couple years later, projected by someone else, those memorable images were all still there, and still striking.

But almost to my surprise, I found that *Easy Rider*, even completely digested, lived up to my broken-mirror-funhouse memories of it. Even today, although somewhat charmingly dated, the film is still audacious, rude, genre-defining—and, unlike a lot of other half-century-old films about which the above could be said—it's also a work of compelling narrative cinema. In short, it's a trip.

None of which, if you are still with me, you need to be told. This book's existence, fifty years down the highway, is testimony to *Easy Rider*'s endurance and popularity, and its ever-widening effect upon Hollywood and the larger weave of popular culture. *Easy Rider* changed Hollywood, but it also changed pop culture, and counterculture, in vast and previously unexplored ways. Many "making-of" books—be they about art or architecture, machines or motorbikes—ignore what happened after those innovative ideas were realized. In other words, those books left *us* and our feelings about these innovations out of the story—wrongly, I think. This is because as much as the story of *Easy Rider* belongs to Peter Fonda and Dennis Hopper (and, more accurately, and legally, to Sony (Columbia) Pictures), it also belongs to the larger world, to us, as well. *Easy Rider: 50 Years Looking for America* tells the story of the making of *Easy Rider*. But it also tells the story of the world that *Easy Rider* made.

I was surprised when at the end of 2018, publisher Rick Rinehart told me, somewhat wistfully, that 2019 would mark the fiftieth anniversary of *Easy Rider*. He said that he would love to publish a book on this subject, but in order for it to actually appear in 2019, it would need to be in the typesetter's hands by April. (Another confession: The above is not an exact quote. Typesetters surely don't have hands in 2019.)

I jumped at the chance—because of the feelings I had about the movie, yes—although I also wondered, frankly, if I could research, write, and complete a full manuscript in such a small amount of time.

Fortunately, I had a lot of help.

First off, I'd like to thank my collaborator, Alan Dunn, a great *Easy Rider* authority, who questioned my assumptions, deleted my errors, and introduced me to the world of *Easy Rider* that exists outside of the film.

I should acknowledge that all four of the primary midwives of *Easy Rider* have excellent biographies already, which I used as jumping-off points. Peter L. Winkler's *Dennis Hopper: The Wild Ride of a Hollywood Rebel*, Patrick McGilligan's *Jack's Life: A Biography of Jack Nicholson*, Lee Hill's *A Grand Guy: The Art and Life of Terry Southern*, and Peter Fonda's own autobiography, *Don't Tell Dad*, are all excellent. I don't personally know any of these gentlemen, but I've liberally quoted them and then adapted some of their conclusions, and I'm grateful to be able to acknowledge their fine works here.

Simon Witter (with Hannes Rossacher) and Nick Ebeling, the respective directors of the terrific documentaries *On the Trail of Easy Rider: 40 Years On . . . Still Searching for America* and *Dennis Hopper: Along for the Ride*, were terrific resources. I'm very grateful for their assistance. In particular, Simon, thank you for air-mailing me a copy of the superlative *On the Trail*, and for letting me use what I saw in it here.

Charlie Ziarko, as always, offered me hardheaded Hollywood insider's advice when I needed it most, and he came up with some interesting *Easy Rider* conclusions, which I can now pretend I thought up by myself. (I still wish I could convince him that *Easy Rider* is a good movie, however.)

I'd also like to acknowledge the contributions, recollections, and reminiscences of Randy Beckstrand, Donn Cambern, George Christie, Donnie "Hair Bear" Derbes, Tom Elliot, Graham Gamble, Jim Griffin, Henry Jaglom, Joyce King, David McGiffert, Blue Miller, Daryl "Caveman" Nelson, Dave Nichols, Mondo Porras, Robert Walker, and Skip Wiatrolik.

I'm also indebted, for various reasons and crimes, to Marilyn Allen, Ron Barblagallo, John Bengston, Albert Coombes, Rob Klein, Joan Ksbosius, Tom Loveman, Jim Pauley, E. J. Stephens, Stephen X. Sylvester, Stan Taffel, Natalie Thompson, and Marc Wanamaker.

My feelings about *Easy Rider* are complex. It bothers my oft-neglected intellectual side that *Easy Rider* still exists mostly as a visceral and misunderstood thing for me, and for a lot of other fans, too. The amount of fan support in the form of art, fiction, and videos, including a mainstream movie created by a super fan called *Easy Rider: The Ride Back*; the T-shirts you can buy online and at cycle shows that say WWPFD? ("What would Peter Fonda do?"); the untold number of replica Captain America and Billy bikes on the road, and in private collections and museums—the fact that all of these things are out there is a tangible testament to *Easy Rider*'s permanent place in the hearts of its fans. The very existence of biker culture in the twenty-first century is, if not entirely the result of *Easy Rider*, certainly an acknowledgment of the film as common ground which bikers of all ages and affiliations can share and appreciate. While it's a movie, unlike any other film out there, it's also a lifestyle.

You can love it. You can hate it. You can even mock it, at your peril. But, like only a few other things in history, *Easy Rider* doesn't belong to poets, or critics, or journalists who tell us what to like. Sure, the film was generally well reviewed and very much well liked when it came out. But like Robin Hood and Blackbeard, Davy Crockett and Harry Houdini, King Kong and John Wayne, *Gone with the Wind* and Elvis Presley, *The Rocky Horror Picture Show* and Princess Diana, *Titanic* and Tupac Shakur, you either get it or you don't, and never will.

Easy Rider is one of those rare things that is personal and beloved to many people—people who just don't give a damn what artists or critics or cultural arbiters might think. This book is for you then, for all those who are in it for the easy haul, or for the long ride. It's for those who can recognize the holy light at the end of the road, even if that light is only recognized as holy by a very few.

See you farther down that road.

—Steven Bingen
Hollywood, California, 2019

Chapter One

The Road to *Rider*

THE ROAD TO *EASY RIDER* BEGAN, OF ALL PLACES, IN A DARK, POT-INFUSED motel room in Toronto, Canada.

It was November 27, 1967. We know this because Peter Fonda, then a young actor of unfulfilled promise, remembers it even today as the date that would change his life.

Fonda, the son of screen legend Henry Fonda, was in Canada to promote his latest picture, *The Trip* (1967), a low-budget counterculture circus, ring-led by low-budget counterculture ringleader Roger Corman. *The Trip* had been scripted by another unlucky actor, Jack Nicholson, and costarred a third underachiever named Dennis Hopper.

One of Fonda's duties in town was to attend a motion picture exhibitors' conference that day. He remembers that Jack Valenti, the keynote speaker, had just been elected president of the Motion Picture Association of America. Peter Fonda also vividly remembers part of the speech Valenti delivered that day.

"My friends—and you are my friends," Valenti began. "It is time we stopped making movies about motorcycles, sex, and drugs!"[1] Fonda, who was involved, and invested in, all three of those deadly sins at the time, remembers thinking that Valenti sounded just like a television evangelist. He had a booming, pipe-organ voice, even sported a rather cornpone Southern accent—like several future participants in our story, Jack Valenti hailed from Texas—and, as if he knew how Fonda felt, throughout his long talk Valenti seemed to be staring right at, right into, the actor.

After that endless, uncomfortable conference, Fonda walked back to the underwhelming Hillcrest Motel, where the notoriously spendthrift Corman was putting him up. Bored and lonely, and admittedly paranoid from the dressing-down he felt he had gotten from Valenti on his makeshift pulpit, Fonda lit a roach and proceeded to get stoned in that motel room.

Amid the pot smoke, Peter Fonda found himself inexplicably mesmerized by an old publicity still from one of his previous films, *The Wild Angels* (1966), which for some reason had been included with *The Trip*'s press kit—probably for him to autograph for some Canadian exhibiter's teenage daughter. The still depicted himself and actor Bruce Dern, with a motorcycle, near Venice Beach, California.

Oddly, perhaps because of his enhanced state, Fonda found himself looking at that photograph through the marijuana smoke and thinking that the picture looked like something from, well, a Hollywood Western. Perhaps it was because the two of them, Fonda and Dern, were almost silhouetted, and how the bike, also nearly silhouetted, seemed to be standing in for a horse. The still had been taken on an asphalt road, but it had been reprinted so many times by Corman's cut-rate photo lab that much of the definition had bled away, so this indistinct copy of a copy looked like it had been taken in an earlier era on a Western street in Tombstone, Arizona, or Deadwood, South Dakota, rather than near the Venice boardwalk. And to him, he and Dern looked for all the world like two lonely Texas cowboys.

Right there, in that smoke-filled room, amid the stacked room-service trays and dirty towels, Peter Fonda decided to make a Western himself. A Western with motorcycles. In fact, Fonda later pitched the story just as he had first envisioned it: as "a modern Western with two hip guys on bikes instead of old movie stars on horses."[2]

In his memoir, Fonda went even further, referring to the story as being "about the Duke and Jeffery Hunter looking for Natalie Wood. I would be the Duke, and Hopper would be my Ward Bond. America would be our Natalie Wood, and after a long journey to the East across John Ford's America, what would become of us? We would be blasted to bits by narrow-minded redneck poachers at dawn, just outside of Heaven, Florida."[3]

In his dreams that night about cowboys on choppers, Fonda probably didn't yet know something his boss, Roger Corman, most likely did—that in fact, the recent trend in "biker movies" was just an outgrowth of a late-1950s trend in Westerns, which Jack Valenti doubtless would have looked upon more approvingly, and which Corman had earlier similarly exploited. After all, the two genres both incorporated huge dollops of masculinity, rugged individualism, action, violence, and a feeling for the open road, paved or not.

More directly, Roger Corman had been inspired to make *The Wild Angels* by a photograph of a biker's funeral, although the subsequent screenplay had also been "unofficially" based on a book, *Hell's Angels: A Strange and Terrible Saga*, written by future celebrity journalist Hunter S. Thompson and published the same year, 1967. The book had been preceded by a controversial magazine article in *The Nation*, also by Thompson, and by a series of other articles and newspaper features which examined the increasingly troubling (to most Americans) increase in motorcycle clubs.

These clubs were originally made up of disillusioned World War II veterans who had returned from combat, and, unable—or unwilling—to reintegrate into society, had subsequently formed their own splinter society, with their own sometimes hedonistic rules and codes of honor. In 1947 a motorcyclist rally in Hollister, California, got out of hand when up to four thousand cyclists (that number has since been widely disputed) virtually took over the tiny city, breaking bottles, joyriding on the streets, damaging public property, and sleeping on citizens' lawns. Hollister's seven-man police force, unsurprisingly, was unable to control the pandemonium (although one witness to the melee reported that the worst violence actually committed against a policeman involved an officer's having his hat stolen, so there may have been some slight subsequent exaggeration about the incident in the press).

The "Hollister riot," as the event has somewhat grandiosely been called, inspired the term *1-percenter*, which refers to a statement issued by the American Motorcyclist Association after the incident, stating that 99 percent of its members were law-abiding citizens. So, being a 1-percenter, then, reflected the true outlaw biker, and became a literal badge of honor among Hells Angels, for example, who still proudly sport "1%" patches on their leathers.

The Hollister riot tale was later fictionalized and dramatized in the film *The Wild One* (1953), which starred Marlon Brando, and which was the first official biker film. *The Wild One* also contained the biker manifesto, as expressed in this dialogue:

Mildred: Hey, Johnny. What are you rebelling against?
Johnny: Whaddya got?

To an even greater degree than the Hollister riot, *The Wild One* was a controversial and unsettling look into the dark side of its era. Today, in the wake of later biker movies, it is interesting to note how the public, and the critics, responded to the biker mythos the first time it was dramatized. In 1953, in spite of the charismatic appeal of the young Brando, most Americans—and, in fact, the filmmakers themselves—seemed to consider bikers to be the spawn of the devil, in vivid contrast to the image of the biker as a "harbinger of a new freedom" which *Easy Rider* would unveil some fifteen years later.

The Wild One, despite its success, failed to start a trend in motorcycle movies. Although Elvis Presley wore a leather jacket and rode a Honda 305cc Superhawk in *Roustabout* (1964), he was not depicted as a "biker." In fact, the only actual biker character who appeared on-screen in a mainstream picture for the next decade was Harvey Lembeck's comedic Eric Von Zipper, in American International's silly but popular Beach Party films.

Roger Corman, whose films were distributed by American International Pictures (AIP), and who knew how to create, spot, or follow a trend better than anyone, probably realized that motorcycles, and crime, and counterculture, would be a good mix—and would be successful, just as his Westerns and horror movies had been earlier.

This led to *The Wild Angels*, in 1966. In addition to starring Fonda and Dern, the film costarred Frank Sinatra's daughter Nancy (casting the younger, cheaper children of celebrities was another trend Corman was exploiting at the time). The film's success, especially in relation to its cramped budget, was extraordinary, although critics would fail to take any biker movie (and there would be a great many to follow) seriously for the next three years.

Another significant influence on *Easy Rider*, although it would not be noted by anyone in particular at the time, was the so-called "road movie." The road movie genre, whose existence would not be apparent except in hindsight, owes its origins to literature. Miguel de Cervantes' *Don Quixote* (1605), is an excellent example of the road movie, without the movie. As the characters in the story travel across a vast and changing landscape and meet up with different people, the resultant text provides social commentary about the characters and those they meet. Mark Twain's *The Adventures of Huckleberry Finn* (1884), Joseph Conrad's *Heart of Darkness* (1902), and John Steinbeck's *The Grapes of Wrath* (1939) have also been anointed as literary road movies, although Jack Kerouac's *On the Road* (1957) is rightly considered to be a more-obvious predecessor to *Easy Rider* than any of the above.

On the big screen, *Wild Boys of the Road* (1933) is one of the earliest (and most raw) road movies, although the more-genial (and successful) *It Happened One Night* (1934) is usually labeled the grandfather of a genre that includes *The Wizard of Oz* (1939), *Stagecoach* (1939), *Detour* (1945), *Two for the Road* (1967), *Bonnie and Clyde* (1967), *Vanishing Point* (1971), *Paper Moon* (1973), *Smokey and the Bandit* (1977), *National Lampoon's Vacation* (1983), *Rain Man* (1988), *Thelma and Louise* (1991), *Green Book* (2018), and dozens of others. Other countries have also contributed notable examples to the genre. Australia, in particular, has a particularly fertile tradition of road movies, as that country, like the United States, contains no shortage of open spaces and open roads.

On television, *Easy Rider*'s obvious predecessor was *Route 66* (1960–1964), which shared with the movie both a love of the landscape and a certain Jack Kerouac–inspired ambivalence about the people who populate that landscape. *Easy Rider* and *Route 66* also both benefited from extensive location shooting, which was particularly rare on television in the 1960s, when even outdoor-genre pieces, like Westerns, tended to be shot largely on soundstages and studio backlots.

In 1967, however, the biker movie and the road movie were running parallel to each other. The two would not swerve into each other's lane and collide until that intoxicated evening in Toronto changed everything forever.

That same intoxicated November evening, Fonda called up his friend, Dennis Hopper. Actually, he woke up Hopper's wife, Brooke Hayward—at three in the morning—and forced her to put her groggy husband on the phone. It should be noted that Peter Fonda and Brooke Hayward had been childhood friends, and Peter had met Dennis at their wedding.

Fonda remembered that in addition to costarring in *The Trip*, Corman had also allowed Hopper to direct some of the second-unit footage for the film. Peter Fonda had been impressed with his friend's visual sense, and even at this embryonic point in our story, already thought that the actor would be a good director for his "Western."

Dennis Hopper (Fonda liked to annoy his friend by calling him "Hoppe," or, even worse, "Den-Den"), like Fonda, was a child of the movies, although he had grown up in Kansas watching them rather than watching them being made. He arrived in Hollywood in 1954, and in 1955, he costarred in *Rebel Without a Cause* opposite James Dean. Actually "costarred" is perhaps the wrong word for Hopper's gang-member bit part in that classic. Nonetheless, James Dean impressed the young actor tremendously, and like many of his generation, Hopper would spend the next decade emulating Dean's personal and professional persona, including following Dean's example of being alienated, difficult on set, and mistrusting of authority figures.

Hopper once rather confusingly admitted, on an episode of *The David Frost Show* (1969–1972), that "whether I was going to keep getting drunk at parties and telling people, you know, how I was going to make a great film for fifteen years, or whether I was going to sit in a chair and figure out if I could get out of that chair, could I make a movie?" So, Fonda's offer, at that moment, must have seemed like a one-shot, do-or-die proposition to an actor who had spent much too much time, by that point in his career, sitting on his hands in that chair.

Hopper later said he was surprised to hear from Fonda, because the two had recently quarreled, as Hopper, like James Dean, tended to do with most of his friends, most of the time. Fonda told Hopper that he had an idea for a picture which at that time he was calling *The Losers*.

Fonda would produce, Hopper could direct, and they would both write and star. Hopper, of course, was enthusiastic. They agreed to talk again, back in Los Angeles.

Once he'd returned to LA himself, Fonda excitedly pitched his idea to his own wife, Susan Brewer. By now he knew that his two lead characters were going to be stunt performers for some sort of car show, that they make a big drug score and set off across the country on their motorcycles, and that because of their long hair, they are not allowed to check into motels, so, they have to camp out, where they tell each other their dreams around the campfire. Fonda described all of this with the same fever-dream intensity he had used in telling his story to Dennis Hopper, but his audience this time received it with less historic results.

"That's the corniest story I've ever heard," Brewer told him, shaking her head.[4]

Fonda, and now Hopper, *loved* the idea, however. Fonda claimed in 1970 to have some silent home movies somewhere of he and Hopper circling each other on Fonda's tennis court, plotting out the movie together. A soundtrack would have been superfluous, because the two of them are obviously making their storytelling points visually. Fonda later recalls, "That movie's funny, man. I'm long and gangly, and he's short and fat, and he's almost, like, *boxing* me out there, and the whole time my daughter Bridget is riding her tricycle in and out and between us, and we don't even see her. And if I come up with a scene, you see Dennis jump up and slap my hand, and when Dennis would come up with a scene—like the lawyer being drunk in jail—I'd do the same thing. That's how we wrote the whole movie,"[5] he remembers.

Almost as impressed with the idea as Dennis Hopper, fortunately, was author Terry Southern, a quintessential player of the 1950s and '60s. Perhaps because of his infamy, he knew, loved, was involved with, fought with, or worked with every important, infamous, notorious person or event or party or movement that occurred or defined or scandalized those decades. In 1967, for example, Southern had just appeared as one of the famous faces in the crowd on the Beatles' *Sgt. Pepper's Lonely Hearts Club Band* album.

It goes without saying that he was also very talented. Paddy Chayefsky, who was not at all modest about his own achievements as an author, begrudgingly admitted that "Terry Southern writes the best dialogue in America." The equally hard-to-please Gore Vidal, likewise, called Southern "the most profoundly witty writer of our generation." And Southern's friend, humorist Michael O'Donoghue, said that "If there were a Mount Rushmore of American satire, Terry Southern would be the mountain they'd carve it from." Finally, not to be outdone, *Texas Monthly* loftily anointed Southern as "the greatest novelist-screenwriter ever to come out of Alvarado [Texas]!"[6]

About the same time he was being immortalized on that very busy record cover, Terry Southern went to Rome to do some rewrites on *Barbarella* (1968), which starred Peter's sister, Jane Fonda. Peter, who like everyone of note during that era already knew Southern slightly, pitched the famous author the story of his biker film while in Italy himself. Fonda was aware that a biker film was far from Southern's usual, satirical comfort zone. And yet, before he had even filled him in on all the details he and Hopper had come up with for their colorful, but rough, road movie, Southern stopped him and bellowed excitedly, "That's the most incredible story I've ever heard!"[7] Flabbergasted, and wondering if he should now try to talk Terry Southern out of this statement, Fonda instead told him that they only needed someone to put the narrative in script form. To which Southern said, "I'm your man."

"You don't understand," Fonda said. "Your fee is the [entire] budget of the movie."

"I'm your man," Southern repeated.[8]

Southern's surprising enthusiasm for the project certainly worked to the film's advantage, but ultimately less so to Southern's own benefit. No one had a clue yet as to what a money machine *Easy Rider* would become, so Southern agreed to $350 per week, which was scale. He ended up being paid the grand sum of $3,900 for his work and for his name, a transparent sliver of the $100,000 per script he was commanding at the time.

The money Southern took and ran with was paltry even by the standards of *Easy Rider*, although, according to his biographer, Lee Hill, Southern did receive long-term residuals from *Easy Rider*—usually $50 to $100 a year! But, as Hill asserts, most other participants at the time made far more money than he. In fact, if he had been offered—and then taken—even a single percentage point, Southern could have continued to finance his extravagant lifestyle through at least some of the lean years ahead.

In 1999, Paul Lewis, *Easy Rider*'s production manager, finally got tired of listening to Terry Southern's fans and friends, who had inflicted martyrdom upon their hero for years regarding his compensation. "Terry Southern *had* points [profit participation] in *Easy Rider*," Lewis wrote in a 1999 letter to the *New Times LA* weekly newspaper, "as did almost everyone artistically or technically involved in making the picture. Terry returned his points for the same reason he wanted his name removed from the writing credit: He didn't feel he had contributed enough to merit them."[9]

Frankly, Terry Southern's importance to *Easy Rider* cannot be overstated, even though his contribution to the *story* has been subsequently—and probably unjustly—minimized, mostly by Dennis Hopper, in the decades after the film's release. In 1969, his name in the titles alone transformed *Easy Rider* from a disreputable biker flick, one which starred three actors who had made more than their share of disreputable biker flicks, into an overt work of cinema that demanded attention. "Why would this guy who was considered [part of the] real *intelligentsia* be with these two creeps unless there was something up?" Fonda has said bluntly.[10]

Southern is also credited with naming the film. "He gave us the title *Easy Rider*. We didn't have that title. That was fabulous," Peter Fonda affirms.[11]

The term *easy rider* originally referred to a horse, which literally was an "easy ride." A more salacious definition came about in the twentieth century as the phrase came to represent a person, usually a woman, of lose sexual mores. In *She Done Him Wrong* (1933), for example, Mae West sings "I Wonder Where My Easy Rider's Gone," which is about exactly what it sounds like it's about. By the 1960s, the phrase had gotten even more specific, referring to a person who was the lover, but not the pimp, of a prostitute. He was there, presumably, for the easy ride, as she did most of the work.

At the time, American International Pictures, which of course had a relationship with Fonda, Hopper, and biker flicks in general, was the obvious easy ride for *Easy Rider*. But Roger Corman and studio heads Samuel Z. Arkoff and James H. Nicholson (who was no relation to Jack Nicholson despite published reports to the contrary) didn't yet seem to realize that the project was suddenly outgrowing their tiny studio. Arkoff objected to the idea of a movie with drug dealers as heroes. To which Fonda replied, "What we're doing is fucking with the rules. There should be no rules, man. We're being honest with ourselves."[12]

Ultimately, AIP offered a deal that would allow Hopper to direct or to costar, but not to do both. Producer Fonda, out of loyalty to his friend, balked at this, so AIP reluctantly agreed to let Hopper both act and direct, no doubt contrary to their better judgment. Fonda finally walked away from the table anyway over a clause which could have removed Hopper from the director's chair if at any time during the production he fell three days behind schedule. "This was not something I was going to agree to," Fonda remembers.[13]

At this point Roger Corman briefly flirted with the idea of financing the film personally himself, but ultimately he declined to participate as well. Jack Nicholson has estimated that this ultimately cost the producer some $26 million! "*Easy Rider* was a good project and [I thought it] would do well. I didn't think it would do *that* well," Corman has said. "It was going to cost between three and four hundred thousand dollars. I was eager to produce it when AIP was backing it, but I was reluctant to put that much money up myself. I had only backed films costing $100,000 or less. Sure, I regret pulling away, but those are the breaks of the game in Hollywood."[14]

Suddenly, and frighteningly, minus financing, a studio, and distribution, *Easy Rider* could have easily toppled into what would later be termed "development hell," and never emerged.

So, as writer Patrick McGilligan has put it, Hopper and Fonda then "tried to wheel and deal their project around Hollywood, without much success. The treatment had large gaps, and Hopper, when he was waving his arms and shouting, his eyes flashing like cherry tops, tended to scare backers."[15]

But somehow, against the odds, *Easy Rider* instead failed upward by landing at one of the largest studios in the world.

Easy Rider's entrée into corporate Hollywood was Bob Rafelson and Bert Schneider's Raybert Productions (founded in 1965). Although at the time Raybert had only produced the successful *Monkees* TV series (1966–1968), that was enough. Because of the *Monkees* money spilling into their coffers, by July of 1968 the company found itself enviably awash in excess cash.

Fonda knew this, and he also knew Rafelson and Schneider slightly, perhaps through Jack Nicholson, who was then working for Raybert as an unlikely producer. Fonda had even shown someone at Raybert (who that was has been disputed) some of his and Hopper's script pages for *Easy Rider*. So, Fonda and Hopper arranged a meeting, in January of 1968, with Rafelson and Schneider, allegedly to talk about a political satire they were kicking around town, to be called *The Queen*.

Just before the crucial Raybert meeting was about to start, however, Hopper wandered out of the waiting room to look for Nicholson (perhaps this was just as well), leaving his partner alone in an office with the two producers, who, in spite of their recent financial windfall, unsurprisingly failed to warm up to *The Queen* (no one ever did).

After an awkward silence, Schneider then asked Fonda how "that motorcycle movie was coming along." Fonda mentioned his problems with AIP, and the fact that he and Hopper believed they could do the whole thing for $350,000. "I was winging it," Fonda admitted.[16]

But Bert Schneider nodded. It was that easy.

Or maybe not. In 2003, Dennis Hopper voiced his suspicion that before the meeting, Jack Nicholson—*Easy Rider*'s behind-the-scenes, and later, in-the-scenes guardian angel—had perhaps prompted Schneider specifically to ask about *Easy Rider*, because of the recent success of biker flicks, and because Nicholson, as a friend to all the parties, believed that Schneider would be receptive.

A few days later, Fonda and Hopper, both of them in the same office at the same time this go-round, signed a deal for which they would receive one-third ownership of *Easy Rider*, and $40,000 "starter money." Fonda found out later that after he had left the office, "Bert asked Bob, 'Can Dennis actually make a film with a beginning, a middle, and an end?'"[17]

The best thing about the deal was that Bert Schneider's father, Abraham, was the president of the mighty Columbia Pictures. In October of 1968, Schneider ultimately sold his old man the picture for $500,000—while it was still in production. Ironically, Columbia had produced *The Wild One* back in 1953, and would now also release *Easy Rider*.

The $40,000 was earmarked by the two partners for a location trip to New Orleans during Mardi Gras, which had been planned as part of the story from the earliest days (reflected by the fact that the project was briefly titled *Mardi Gras*). Fonda, already learning to be a producer, realized that just by showing up and pointing their cameras at the crowds and colors and revelries there, they would achieve a lot of classy production value without having to pay a cent for any of it.

The idea was for Fonda and Hopper, accompanied by a few friends—along with Karen Black and Toni Basil, whom they had cast as the two hookers Hopper and Fonda's characters drop acid with—to show up, and then to just film whatever happened, *cinema verité* style, using lightweight 16mm equipment. Hopper even went to New Orleans for a "scouting trip." Unfortunately, producer Fonda got the dates mixed up as to when exactly Mardi Gras was, so the crew had to scramble to arrive in late February 1968, while the celebration was still going on.

That "crew," made up of enthusiastic, soon-to-be-accomplished friends, was eclectic indeed. It included the documentarian Les Blank, character actor Seymour Cassel, production manager Alan Pariser, another actor, Richard Rust, and at least three actual (or future) cinematographers: Peter Pilafian, Baird Bryant, and Barry Feinstein. The ever-bemused Terry Southern apparently thought the whole experience would be a lark, so he showed up as well, rather mysteriously.

At the motel parking lot in New Orleans, Hopper assembled his eager crew on the first morning and proceeded to deliver a paranoid, expletive-riddled diatribe about how this was *his* movie, and how *no one* was going to take it away from him. This pep talk lasted for two hours, while Fonda impatiently worried about how much of the Mardi Gras festivities they had come two thousand miles to record they were missing. Production finally started at 11:30 a.m. It was February 23, 1968—Peter Fonda's twenty-eighth birthday.

Karen Black later recalled this day (and the following four), saying, "Dennis was afraid that if we got too far away from him physically, that he would have an idea, and that we wouldn't be there to shoot his idea. So, he would say, 'Are you there? Are you there? Are you there?' We'd say 'Yes. What do you want us to do?' He'd say, 'I don't know, I don't know . . .'"[18]

Hopper warned his "cameramen" not to shoot anything without his consent, and then would get manic when he would see his auteurs filming clouds or puddles or parades. Everyone there had ambitions to direct, or to shoot, and so they did, to the detriment of their actual director.

In the evenings, the crew would tiredly gather in someone's hotel room to try to figure out what exactly their director wanted from them the next day. Hopper, instead of telling them, would launch into yet another exhaustive monologue, which would raise additional questions rather than answer any, leaving his alleged crew still shaking their heads. One night, Black remembers that Terry Southern, the company gadfly, languidly told the director that "The cacophony of your verbiage is driving me to slumber." In response, Hopper could only think to repeatedly sputter "Oh, really? The cacophony, huh? The cacophony, huh? The cacophony, huh?,"[19] until everyone finally went back to their own rooms to sleep, still unsure about the following day.

One night, early in the shoot, Hopper decided that he absolutely *had* to run outside with one of the cameras and film some cool neon signs out in the hotel parking lot. But Barry Feinstein, not surprisingly, didn't want to give his director the camera, which was his, and which he was afraid Hopper might damage. The two of them somehow got into a fight, a noisy, physical punching and shoving match, which climaxed with their crashing through the door of Basil and Black's room. Peter Fonda was there, entertaining the girls with Black's guitar, which Hopper promptly smashed over Feinstein's head. The director then picked up the TV set and threw it, again at Feinstein, before falling facedown into the coffee table.

Fonda picked up his sleeping partner and dragged him onto a bed (no one remembers whose bed it was), and then pulled off his cowboy boots and socks. At this, Den-Den abruptly sat upright. His eyes popped open.

"Don't ever take off my boots again," he slurred. His last bit of direction for the night before finally falling asleep.

The Mardi Gras scenes which Fonda had wanted so badly were largely a bust. There are only a handful of grainy shots of the cast in the parade or out on the street. It's even been reported (but never confirmed) that some of the Mardi Gras material was made up after the fact from stock footage pilfered from another production. "When the Saints Go Marching In" even plays on the soundtrack here, as if to confirm to the audience that this is, in fact, actually Mardi Gras. Later, however, away from those crowds and time constraints, and having relocated to a secluded cemetery, Hopper was able to indulge in his Jean-Luc Godard–inspired penchant for non-narrative, nonlinear cinema for the final two days of the shoot.

These scenes were shot at what is still called the St. Louis Cemetery No. 1 in New Orleans, which opened in 1789 in the city's beloved French Quarter. No one bothered to ask permission of the Catholic Church before the crew showed up, and apparently the church was not happy with the assorted desecrations and humiliations that took place amid the graves, which Hopper's cameras documented. In 2014, the Archdiocese of New Orleans closed the cemetery to the general public—and to *Easy Rider* fans—after Voodoo Priestess Marie Laveau's tomb, which was nearby, was repeatedly vandalized.

Hopper still had trouble controlling his associates, who by now had taken to disappearing behind buildings or tombstones or quitting in frustration. In one case, at least, the inexperience of his minions gave him an interesting effect. Les Blank accidentally opened up an exposed film magazine, slightly fogging the images inside and resulting in a curious hazy ambiance which Hopper was completely thrilled with.

When the crew got back to Hollywood, Fonda, frustrated with Hopper's megalomaniacal performance in the Big Easy, had a talk with William "Bill" Hayward, whom he and Hopper together had hired as an associate producer. Hayward, uncomfortably, was the brother of Brooke

Hayward, who was married to—but now estranged from—Dennis Hopper. The two of them decided to take their concerns to Bert Schneider.

Fonda also confided his fears to Brooke Hayward. Brooke's mother was actress Margaret Sullavan, who had once been married to Henry Fonda, so the two already had more than just Dennis Hopper standing between them. He told her that "the footage is going to be dreadful; the whole thing is awful, it's a disaster."[20] Peter also told Brooke his fear that Dennis Hopper might have to be fired.

A screening of the 25,000 feet of New Orleans material was arranged, and sure enough, the footage was, as Bill Hayward unpromisingly called it, "an endless parade of shit."[21] Brooke Hayward agreed. "It was just dreadful stuff, murky, the camerawork wasn't any good," she recalled. "The talent I know Dennis had, and Peter knew Dennis had—that we'd seen in the second-unit stuff for *The Trip* that he'd shot—none of it was there. There was a terrible silence in the screening room."[22]

Brooke Hayward, it must be said, had never been a fan of the film. She had goaded Hopper on the way to the airport for his ill-fated Mardi Gras trip by telling him that "this is never going to work. Peter can't act. I've known him since I was a child. You're just going to make a fool of yourself."[23]

Dennis Hopper's dream of getting out of that chair and proving her wrong seemed to be crumbling before his eyes.

Fonda and Bill Hayward eventually agreed that the honorable thing to do would be to offer to let Raybert out of its deal, and to let Pando Productions, Fonda's newly formed company, refund that squandered $40,000, which they offered to do. Fonda even contritely said that he would be willing to step aside and let Schneider personally produce *Easy Rider* himself.

Instead, Schneider asked Fonda if he still wanted to make the movie, to which Fonda replied that he most certainly did. Then, surprisingly, Schneider quietly told Fonda to get out of his office and go out and make it.

Hopper later remembered those days. "I get back, and unbeknownst to me, Peter and Bill Hayward, my brother-in-law, came back from New Orleans and offered to give back the $20,000 [*sic*], that obviously,

I was a crazy person. And what they had done, they started taping my screaming and my ranting and raving, and they played this for Bert Schneider and Jack Nicholson, and Bert said, 'Well, he sounds excited, but you know what—I hired this person to direct this movie. He's going to direct this movie.'"[24]

There would, of course, be some stipulations. For one thing, no more guerrilla tactics with friends. From now on, for the entire seven-week shoot, the production would get serious, with 35mm film; schedules, permits, and budgets; and a fully unionized crew. Schneider assumed (rightly, as it turned out) that Hopper would have a harder time bullying and browbeating such a crew, which would also be more likely, and better able, to give their director what he needed to realize his perhaps-crazed vision.

Most importantly, they hired László Kovács as the film's cinematographer. Kovács, born in Hungary, had launched his Hollywood career shooting low-budget exploitation films, including, significantly, grisly biker pictures like *Hells Angels on Wheels* (1967), a genre which he was most certainly not anxious to return to. Hopper, however, immediately saw that Kovács was the only man for the job. Fonda saw that Kovács would work cheaply and quickly, and presumably get along well with his director. Which he did.

Most of the rest of the crew came out of the ranks of exploitation filmmaking as well. Many of those they hired had already worked with Fonda, or Hopper, or each other, before—which meant that they could be counted on to do their jobs quickly and economically. Most importantly, they could be counted on to bond as a unit over the course of what promised, it goes without saying, to be a very difficult and unusual shoot.

CHAPTER TWO

Inside and Outside

THE FIRST IMAGE ON-SCREEN—AFTER THE COLUMBIA LOGO, AND APTLY enough—is two motorcycles pulling up in front of something called the La Contenta Bar. The bikes are not the motorcycles used in the rest of the movie, but the bikers riding into frame are in fact Peter Fonda and Dennis Hopper, although they are not wearing the costumes they will wear for the rest of the movie.

Fonda, who is wearing a green windbreaker, plays a character usually referred to as "Captain America," although his name in the credits, and the one time it is used on camera, is Wyatt. Hopper, here clad in a sheepskin coat, is Billy. The more-famous outfits they change into when they hit the road—Billy's fringed buckskins and Captain America's leather and American flag ensemble, with boots and spurs—are actually *supposed* to be costumes. It's only mentioned once in the film, but Billy and Wyatt are actually performers in some sort of stunt show, and Captain America is only the name of the character Wyatt plays in that show.

This puts the concept embraced by so many over the years in jeopardy from virtually the very first shot. The heroes of *Easy Rider* are not really bikers or outlaws at all; they are actually two circus performers who *play* bikers and outlaws.

Fonda—or Southern, or Hopper, or whoever came up with the names for the characters—obviously intended to evoke Billy the Kid and Wyatt Earp (a character Fonda's father had memorably played in 1946's *My Darling Clementine*). Hopper once remarked about the

Western iconography in *Easy Rider* that "this is all very Gary Cooper to me." But his cowboy persona here is a role, just like Fonda's Captain America alias is.

Actually, Billy was supposed to have a nickname, just like Wyatt did. Twice in the film, he is referred to by Captain America as "Bucky." Bucky Barns, of course, was Captain America's sidekick in the Marvel comic-book series. Columbia's lawyers, weary of potential legal action, however, insisted that Fonda overdub "Bucky" with "Billy" in postproduction, which he did.

We learn very little about their pasts, but there are indications that Wyatt and Billy were, before their show business careers had ended, part of the very society the film appears to question. Wyatt, inexplicably and intriguingly, wears on his jacket a Secretary of Defense Department identification badge, which hints at his once working for . . . the man. (In reality, the badge was a gag gift from Fonda's friend, actor Larry Hagman.) And in one early scene, shot in Ballarat, California, Captain America takes off his wristwatch and throws it away. The fact that up until this moment he still owned a watch indicates that he is only at this moment "dropping out."

Nor are our heroes hippies. In fact, although the story is populated by hippies, the word itself is never actually evoked. Wyatt and Billy are outsiders even in the counterculture—and somewhat older outsiders as well. They both appear to be in their late twenties here (Hopper was thirty-three at the time, although he sometimes claimed to be thirty-one at the time of filming, and Fonda was twenty-eight), and their whimsical costumes evoke comic books rather than counterculture. Only Billy's scraggly hair and Wyatt's sideburns, and those motorcycles, alienate them from traditional American society.

Incidentally, Fonda wore his Captain America ensemble and drove his flag-emblazoned motorcycle around Los Angeles for a week before the film started shooting, and was repeatedly harassed by the police.

Dropping out in this context seems to involve dealing cocaine and then taking the money to retire on, which is why our heroes are at the La Contenta. The building these scenes were shot at is still there, in Taos, New Mexico, although currently vacant.

Cocaine was used not because of the shock value inherent in the use of a "scary drug," which is what coke was considered to be at the time, but to smooth out a logistical hiccup. Billy and Wyatt would have had to pull up to the meeting pulling a tractor-trailer in order to have enough marijuana to make $50,000. The uninitiated might also assume that it is unreasonable for two apparently unaffiliated bikers to somehow manage to score such a major drug deal, apparently right under the noses of the Hells Angels, who it might be imagined would have been involved in any such deal undertaken in Los Angeles during this era—although the truth is that this would not necessarily have been the case in the late 1960s.

The cocaine is sold to none other than Phil Spector, a record producer who in real life is currently imprisoned for second-degree murder in the death of his wife, actress Lana Clarkson. Spector took the part as a favor to Hopper, and even allowed them to use his $25,000 limousine and driver-bodyguard (Mac Mashourian) for the scene where Billy and Wyatt get the cash for their cocaine, smuggled in motorcycle batteries. (Powdered sugar was used to portray the drug in the film, which Fonda remembers as being horrible to snort.)

These scenes encompassed the first day of non–New Orleans shooting, set at the edge of the Los Angeles International Airport. At the time, jets used to take off right in front of a tiny public road at the edge of a runway, something which would probably not be allowed today. Fonda remembers driving on this road in earlier days and thinking how dramatic it would be to film a scene for a movie there, with jets blasting across the sky as a backdrop.

The sequence is staged silently, probably because the incessant jet noise would have made it impossible to record usable audio there anyway. According to Fonda, a train full of military equipment on its way to Vietnam also rattled by in the background during one shot, which subsequently was not used. "We decided not to use it in the film because we didn't want to discuss the war," Fonda recalls.[25]

The pickup truck Wyatt and Billy are next seen driving contains two tarped motorcycles, which audiences who know the movie assume contains the bikes the characters will drive for the rest of the movie, and for the rest of their lives.

Not true. The cycles in that truck are actually the scrambler bikes seen in the opening scene. Captain America's cycle, if one cares to apply the proper logic, would have never fit into a pickup, and the handlebars would have hung right over the top of the cab! The first money shot of the actual bikes comes soon, however. Editor Donn Cambern still recalls his impressions fifty years later: "That first look at those machines themselves! How beautiful Peter's machine was, and Dennis's, but primarily Peter's . . . so extraordinary."[26]

"The Pusher" by Steppenwolf is the first song in the movie. The lyrics, ironically, are very critical of the drug-dealing lifestyle which our anti-heroes are about to become a part of. It is played under Billy and Wyatt hiding their booty in Wyatt's gas tank, adorned with the American flag, conceived by Fonda as symbolically "stuffing money into the flag." The scene was shot in Ballarat, only twenty miles from Barker Ranch in Death Valley, where in a few months cult leader Charles Manson would be apprehended, somewhat eerily illustrating the other side of hippie culture and tying *Easy Rider* to yet another, infinitely darker, 1960s touchstone.

Now in their soon-to-be familiar costumes, they set off on their odyssey. As mentioned, these costumes are a buckskin coat and cowboy hat for Billy, and a leather jacket and pants for Captain America. According to Fonda, the idea of a flag on that jacket was borrowed from a John Wayne World War II picture, *Flying Tigers* (1942), in which Wayne's leather jacket, rather ironically, is emblazoned with a Chinese nationalist flag, with Chinese characters, to identify him to the Chinese as an enemy of the Japanese.

More famous even than their ensembles, of course, were the character's motorcycles. "Harley-Davidson wouldn't give us any," Dennis Hopper said. "We asked for bikes to be comped, and they wouldn't comp us any bikes at all. As a matter of fact, they didn't want their image to be an outlaw image, so we had to get some old police bikes and chop 'em up."[27] The four motorcycles (playing the two bikes) in *Easy Rider* are all 1200cc Harley-Davidson Hydra-Glides, "one 1950, two '51s, and a '52,"[28] according to Peter Fonda. Ironically, buying used police motorcycles was also a common practice at the time among the Hells Angels and other biker gangs.

Hopper doesn't mention that the "we" in the above transaction actually referred to one Cliff "Soney" Vaughs (the variant spelling of "Sonny" courtesy of Vaughs's mother), who on behalf of the production, purchased all four of the cycles for $500 each.

A noted motorcycle builder, black activist, and local filmmaker/cameraman, Cliff Vaughs also happened to be an acquaintance of Peter Fonda, who sometimes showed up at Vaughs's house in West Hollywood to talk motorcycles. It was on one of these visits that Fonda, accompanied by Hopper, spotted a tapestry on the wall depicting Mae West, which included the printed song title "I Wonder Where My Easy Rider's Gone," which, as noted earlier, was a prototypical use of the term *easy rider*. So, perhaps it was this tapestry, and Vaughs, and not Terry Southern that sparked the film's ultimate title. Or perhaps not.

Fonda, perhaps beholden to Vaughs for his film's title (or again, perhaps not), did, for one reason or another, hire Vaughs as an associate producer and cycle sitter early in the production. But most mysteriously, Vaughs was ultimately uncredited in the finished film, for reasons which have been variously reported as either being related to objections by Columbia, or because Hopper instead wanted to use his friend, Tex "Red Dog" Hall, as the lead motorcycle wrangler.

Vaughs arranged to have these old police bikes chopped in January of 1968, "with the help of seven guys from Watts," Peter Fonda has said.[29] But, more specifically, Vaughs hired Ben ("Benny") Hardy, an already legendary customizer in the black community, to mold those bikes into the very unique creations ultimately seen in the film.

The distinctive stars-and-bars paint job on Fonda's bike was done by artist Dean Lanza, following Fonda's directive to "make it look just like Captain America's shield." Almost everything else was chromed. "Peter and I sat down and talked to him [Hardy], and Peter designed his, and I did my 'Billy Bike,'" Hopper remembered. "I thought of mine as a more practical, more workable hog."[30]

Mechanic Larry Marcus recalls that "Peter came by the house by himself mostly—Dennis didn't come around as much—and once he asked if there was anything else he could do to help. He was impatient to see the bikes finished. I handed him a nine-sixteenths wrench, and he looked at the bike, then the wrench, then the bike, and just walked off. I don't know why he would go on national TV and tell people he designed or built the bikes; he didn't have anything to do with them."[31] To Hopper's credit, however, and somewhat at odds with his earlier statement, Marcus has also been quoted as saying, "I worshipped the ground Dennis Hopper walked on—he was an extremely talented guy—but I never got along with Peter."[32]

Even if he wasn't exactly handing the wrenches to Marcus either, Peter Fonda did have some very dramatic ideas about how he wanted *his* cycle to look. "I got this crazy idea to stretch mine out and rake it out 45 degrees. Looked great. Uh-huh. The seat is just there on the frame. There's *no* padding," Fonda admitted.[33]

Associate producer Bill Hayward also remembered how uncomfortable being an easy rider really is. "The California chopper, of which [the film's bikes] are representative, was all about style. It made no sense at all. The bikes that they're based on, the Harley-Davidson police bike . . . they didn't have a rear suspension, but they had an amazing seat suspension. The seat took all the abuse! You were semi-protected from the vagaries of the highway by this seat. But of course, the stylistic thing was to get this seat as close as you could to the frame of the bike so you could get as low as possible and have that kind of look . . . so they took away the one thing that saved you from losing your back altogether. There were a lot of guys who used to ride those things that can't even begin to ride a motorcycle today. . . . They weren't motorcycles that you'd go back and forth across the country on. Nobody tried that, I don't think. There must be some nutcases that did, but no rational human being tried it."[34]

It wasn't just the placement of the seat that made the bike difficult; the cycle contained no front brake, turn signals, speedometer, front fender, or horn. "It was a bitch to ride that machine, especially slow," Fonda agreed. "That long front end."[35]

Actually, serious motorcycle aficionados would disagree. Mondo Porras ("Mondo is what everybody calls me, okay?") at the legendary (among hard-core bikers) Denver's Choppers in Reno, Nevada, says that it was actually the rigid front end on the *Easy Rider* bikes that made them so hard to sit on and navigate. "It's all in the engineering," he says. "I have a friend who drives a Springer bike with a front end which is thirty inches over stock. The bikes in *Easy Rider* were maybe fifteen inches! This friend put ninety thousand miles on it over twenty-one months. So, don't try to tell me choppers aren't for long-distance riding!"[36]

So, okay—it was Vaughs, and Hardy, and perhaps Fonda, and even perhaps, to a lesser extent, Hopper, who gave the world those bikes. But, to be fair, it was mostly Ben Hardy.

"Benny was the guy that most people don't know about, but he built the two most famous bikes in the history of motorcycling," said Sugar Bear, another bike customizer. "Had the circumstances been different— had [Hardy] been, maybe, a white guy—he would have been, maybe, an icon. I think that movie influenced more people in motorcycles than anything [else] that has ever happened. The fact that they were built by a black man, I'm proud of that. It would have been nice [if] other people had known—that other people are proud of that. . . . You have to explain to me why the guy that did the two most famous motorcycles in the world is unknown . . . can you see someone saying they didn't know Michelangelo did the Sistine Chapel? No one ever said that he did it. It's there, but no one knows who did it! I mean, come on!"[37]

Vaughs and Marcus (and Marcus, by the way, was white) were very taken by an *Easy Rider* scene, not used, in which Captain America and Billy break down along the road someplace and are promptly surrounded by a menacing-looking gang of black bikers, presumably members of the Chosen Few, a mostly black bike club. It turns out that these cyclists only want to offer assistance. Vaughs said that the scene was cut after he was fired, leaving the final film largely minority-free. According to Paul d'Orléans in his book, *The Chopper: The Real Story*, Cliff Vaughs much regretted the scene's ultimate excision, as he felt it captured "the reality of chopper riding in LA at the time. Had that sequence not been deleted, it might have altered the perception in the years after *Easy Rider* that choppers were solely a white man's game, and the cloud of racist associations hovering around this 'folk art' motorcycle style might have been cleared away."[38]

Unfortunately, as much as one *wants* this scene to be in the movie, no one else remembers it. Donn Cambern and Henry Jaglom, two of the film's editors, have said that they never got to see it; Jaglom has said that if he had, they probably would not have cut it.

The single trace of black consciousness remaining in the film involves Billy and Wyatt driving through the Deep South and waving at some black sharecroppers who wave back tentatively. Paul Warshow, in *Sight and Sound*, noted this tiny scene in 1969, and asked, "[I]f our heroes actually stopped in any of these black homes, or found themselves in a black ghetto in the same way they find themselves in, as it were, a 'redneck ghetto,'... would they be given a feeling of friendship or solidarity?"[39]

Fonda enjoyed motorcycles and appreciated the biker lifestyle, but Hopper, as he admitted, "was *terrified* of the things. So, when I made the movie, every time a shot was done, that bike went right back on the truck."[40]

In spite of Hopper's admitted concerns, he was not, by anyone's definition, the green and novice biker he has been unjustly portrayed as by some. For example, Jeffrey Thomas, who is Bill and Brooke Hayward's nephew—and who, from all indications, never saw the *Easy Rider* set, or perhaps even the film itself—has often told friends over dinner about how "Fonda and Hopper were so out of their element on them, that they couldn't go faster than five mph without losing control. So, they shot the motorcycle journey close-ups with Fonda and Hopper riding on a flatbed truck."[41]

Even the most casual viewing of the film, of course, makes rubbish of this claim. Hopper, for example, was proficient enough to perform some amusing stunts on-camera while astride his mount. In one scene, Billy even stands up on one foot, *while driving*, and then expertly hops back onto the seat of his Billy bike again.

Late in Hopper's career, when he was filming the retro biker flick *Hell Ride* (2008), the filmmakers were worried that Hopper, then in his early seventies, would not be able to operate the vintage Indian motorcycle his character had to ride. His costar Michael Madsen remembered that "the first day on the set, in Barstow . . . they said, 'Do you think he can really ride?' [Hopper] came onto the set and walked over to the bike, and everyone got all quiet. Then he got on it, and kicked it over, and started riding around in a circle. He was the real deal."[42]

For the record, most of the bike travel scenes were shot at 20 to 25 mph—fast enough to look like the drivers were not nervous novices, only nursing their bikes along, but slow enough to keep those beautiful American vistas behind those drivers from blurring.

Peter Fonda has remembered that he and Den-Den would get bored of nursing it along on top of such powerful machines, at so far below the posted speed limits, so occasionally, and just for the hell of it, they would "screw it on," leaving the blinking camera crew behind in their exhaust. Fonda won these impromptu races every time because of the Captain America's long front end, which was more aerodynamic—although the actor's longer arms and legs would force him to put his boots back and lie as flat on the tank as he could in order to leave Hopper's Billy bike behind.

During one scene in a national park, production manager Paul Lewis secured the necessary permits and hired two local policemen to ride in front of the bikes. When the scene was in the can and the crew had pulled over to prepare for the next setup, one of the amused policemen called over the filmmakers to listen to a report coming in over his radio. Apparently, a terrified spectator had called the authorities, frantically telling them that he had seen two policemen being chased by two hippies on motorcycles, themselves being chased by a carload of gangsters with a camera, which the witness somehow mistook for a machine gun, mounted on their hood!

The crew working on *Easy Rider* might have been unionized, but most of them were already all too familiar with the edgy guerrilla tactics of Roger Corman and other exploitation filmmakers. They were well acquainted with how to shoot cheaply and quickly out on the streets, as opposed to their brethren working in air-conditioned soundstages back in Hollywood. Joyce King, *Easy Rider*'s script supervisor, recalled even five decades on that there were usually no bathrooms on the "set." Later, Columbia Pictures, which was held more accountable by the unions than an upstart like AIP would have been, had to settle some labor violations brought up against *Easy Rider* by the Hollywood locals before the movie could be released with a union seal.

Fonda and Hopper are first seen riding their hogs under "Born to Be Wild," the most famous song on this—or arguably any other—

soundtrack. Steppenwolf, the band that recorded it, had been founded only the year before. "My father started playing that album incessantly," actress Illeana Douglas remembers. "I don't remember any other songs on it. Were there any other songs on that album? For that matter, did Steppenwolf even have any other songs, ever?"[43] Actually, to answer Illeana's question, both this song and "The Pusher" had been requisitioned for the film off of that self-titled debut album.

"Born to Be Wild" has the distinction of playing partially under the opening credits of the film, eight minutes into the narrative. (It was very rare, even more so then, than now, to delay the "opening" credits of a mainstream film for such a long time.) The explosive resultant montage of the road, the bikes, and the music is easily one of the most recognized, and parodied, sequences anywhere in popular culture. It also succeeds immediately in hooking the audience, which might not have been particularly invested in a story of two opportunistic drug dealers up to this point. But those familiar chords, edited to the imagery, immediately win over any viewer—at least, any viewer who has ever longed to "head out on the highway." The result is iconic, intoxicating, stirring, and mythic.

It also deserves mention that "Born to Be Wild" represents the first use of the term *heavy metal* in rock 'n' roll history, as in "Heavy metal thunder, racing with the wind." The song, as written, originally had nothing to do with motorcycles. Songwriter Mars Bonfire actually wrote it about his first car, in Ontario, Canada. "He's up there driving a Gremlin," Fonda laughs. "This is what the genesis of 'get your motor running' is all about, this little green Gremlin car! It's hysterical, but perfect."[44]

The adrenaline rush the visuals and the song create is dissipated immediately by a scene where Billy and Wyatt pull into a roadside motel, the Pine Breeze Inn, and the manager turns on the NO VACANCY sign as soon as he sees their bikes and their hair. So much for living off the grid.

Consequently, they are forced to camp out in a gutted farm building, which leads them to a farmer, played by veteran New York actor Warren Finnerty, who allows them to fix a flat tire while he shoes his horse (significantly, frightened by the motorcycle). Once again, the comparison with Hollywood Westerns is obvious here, although Spanish director

Luis Buñuel, one of Hopper's influences, is also effectively (if not very subtly) evoked.

In spite of his Broadway cred, Finnerty, who had recently costarred with Hopper in *Cool Hand Luke*, looks every bit the impoverished dirt farmer he portrays, partially because of his earnest, understated performance, and partially because Hopper forced him to play the role without his dentures. The result is that the actor, only in his mid-forties at the time, appears not to be an actor at all, but rather an authentic old farmer who had perhaps been conscripted on location to play a version of himself. In actuality, it is the rancher's farmhand assistant who is the actual property owner, and who admitted to the crew that he had been notified shortly before their arrival that his son had been killed in Vietnam.

Fonda's Captain America has one of the best—and one of the most understated—lines in the film here, when he tells Finnerty that "It's not every man that can live off the land, you know. You do your own thing in your own time. You should be proud." Twenty-five years later, in his reevaluation of the film, critic Roger Ebert noted how "the rancher, who might understandably have replied, 'Who the fuck asked you?,' nods gratefully."[45]

The Byrds' "I Wasn't Born to Follow" pushes the narrative into the next road montage, which introduces Luke Askew's enigmatic hitchhiker character, also known, pointlessly, as the "Stranger on the Highway." Askew was another *Cool Hand Luke* alumnus, and brings a touch of humor to his mysterious hippie character, a cliché even in 1969. Check out the following dialogue:

Billy: I just want to know where you're from.

Stranger on the Highway: The city.

Billy: You're from the city?

Stranger on the Highway: It doesn't make any difference what city; all cities are alike. That's why I'm out here now.

Billy: That's why you're out here now? Why?

Stranger on the Highway: 'Cause I'm from the city—a long way from the city; and that's where I wanna be right now.

So, why exactly *doesn't* the Stranger just tell them what city he's from?

At a gas station Askew pumps petrol into Captain America's flag-decorated tank, which of course is filled with their illegal haul. This worries the paranoid Billy, who is afraid that the drifter will find it. Fonda reassures his sidekick that it's all right, and when they try to pay for the gas, Askew reassures Fonda that "that's all taken care of." Which is a nice touch of solidarity, although it's hard not to wonder when Askew paid for the gas, because he is never actually seen doing so.

With Askew's character riding behind Captain America, the little group crosses into Monument Valley accompanied by The Band's iconic "The Weight." Visually these are the most beautiful images in a film filled with beautiful images.

On the afternoon this scene was shot, as was usually the case, and would continue to be true for the rest of the shoot, the crew was running behind schedule. So, on the evening when they got to the location, the light was already nearly gone. Kovács warned Hopper there was not enough illumination to shoot. Hopper screamed at him to open up the lens two stops and shoot it anyway, which the cinematographer did, under protest.

Hopper's hunch was right.

"That was my greatest motorcycle experience, going across this canyon and catching this light for this shot," Hopper remembered, decades later.[46] "John Ford's America," he called the iconic imagery they recorded during the distant Western twilight. Although it is ironic, if one cares to consider it, that *these* wayward Westerners are going east. "I was trying to make something that looked like a Western, with a kind of Western morality. With the two outlaws who come into town, and everybody's suspicious of them and what they're about. They ride on, camping out, the motorcycles are like the horses, the commune becomes like the old town," Hopper recalled in 2009.[47]

The beautiful footage Kovács conjured for his director on that long-ago evening certainly does evoke John Ford, but, unlike anything else which has been shot in Monument Valley *since* Ford, Hopper manages to reference, not mimic, the work of the master. Perhaps because *Easy Rider* was not—on the surface, anyway—a Western, it manages here to make the location's iconic buttes and canyons and sunsets speak to *these* characters, about them and their doomed quest, rather than just evoke, once again, Ford's many last stands and lost causes created on this site.

At this point, the film has certainly succeeded in creating a very lyrical mood, probably the first time such a word could be used to describe a biker movie. The mood is sustained even into the following scene, set again at a campsite, with the three drifters discussing the future and saying "like" and "man" a lot of times.

The next day the travelers arrive at their hitchhiker's commune. The scenes before they enter the compound were shot in Taos, New Mexico, which Hopper would soon make his home, but the lodge and grounds were constructed for the film in the Santa Monica Mountains above Los Angeles. It "was the only set we ever built," Hopper recalled.[48] When the bikers dismount, Askew amusingly, and with great ceremony, washes his armpits in a communal basin without taking off his jacket! "It was just something funny to do," he recalled in 1995. "I felt the movie was taking itself so seriously that I had to harpoon it."[49] In a cowboys and Indians game, Billy plays with the local children, who "shoot" him, foreshadowing the film's climax.

Many of the extras in this sequence were played by actual hippies, recruited from nearby Topanga Canyon in exchange for a place to flop and meals while the shoot was going on ("lots of beans," Fonda remembers). So, the make-believe commune constructed just for the movie ended up, at least briefly, becoming the real thing.

Among the actual hippies were also some significant faces, either through the benefit of hindsight, or because of their then-relationships to the principals. Fonda's son, three-year-old Justin, can be seen (and heard), crying, in red coveralls. His daughter, five-year-old Bridget, later a film star herself, is there as well, as is the children's' mother, Susan Brewer. Another future star, Carrie Snodgress, apparently wanders through, and Dan Haggerty, the eventual *The Life and Times of Grizzly Adams* TV celebrity, who at the time was working as a motorcycle expert and stuntman, is seen seeding the communal garden (the "seeds" he throws are actually easier-to-photograph dirt and rocks). Famed experimental "assemblage" artists Wallace Berman and George Hermes, who Hopper admired greatly, are apparently somewhere in this scene as well, although not recognizably.

Also among the commune dwellers is Sabrina Scharf, who would run and lose a bid for the California State Senate in 1976. A larger role is taken by Luana Anders, a lifelong friend of Jack Nicholson's (Nicholson thanked her in his acceptance speech when he won an Oscar in 1988), who plays the hippie, Lisa, who Captain America proceeds to hang with. Actress/producer Helena Kallianiotes, another Nicholson crony, is also visible here.

Robert Walker Jr. (billed on-screen as Robert Walker) was actually the look-alike son of the famous leading man from the 1940s–'50s era (his mother was movie star Jennifer Jones). He plays the supposed leader of the hippie cult. Walker offers a communal prayer, and beseeches God to give them a "place to make a stand," another Western analogy, while Hopper's camera effectively pans in a circle around his followers. Walker recalls:

My agent said that Fonda and Hopper had gotten in touch with him. I knew them both. I also knew Rafelson—his wife was really good friends with my wife at the time. They wanted me to be a part of this movie they were doing. It was only a day's work. They were paying everybody five hundred dollars a day. Lots of friends were going to be in it, even some of my family members; my wife came, my two little kids were there. It was just a labor of love. I said, sure, I'll do it. Just a chance to get together and party with friends.

We did the prayer scene first. It took forever. Dennis had it in his head to do this 360-degree pan. We're all standing around in this little Quonset hut type thing. It took forever; we couldn't sit down, had to stand there in the heat for hours. Technically, it was a difficult shot. They had a very tough time with it. In the meantime, they were puffing bee smoke into our faces, because they wanted the atmosphere. We were all truly suffering and struggling for breath. When it finally came time for me to offer my prayer, I could barely speak.

Anyway, we did the darn thing, and then we broke for lunch, and that was it. I was told they were finished with me. Now everyone that wasn't working was standing around, smoking this kind of dope and that kind of dope, hash and pot and whatever. But I'd stayed away from everything until then because I had to work. I always took the work seriously. But when they said I was through, I said, "Oh, right—time to party a little." So, I went around and sampled a little of everybody's wares. Soon, very soon, I was stoned out of my gourd!

Then Dennis came up to me and said, "You know a little tai chi, right?" I was mortified, because I had just started doing tai chi. Just started. Now I'm seriously into it, but at the time I didn't know what I was doing. And remember, I was stoned! But Dennis said, "Just get up there and do it!" I did—but what I did was horrible. You can't even recognize it as tai chi.[50]

Looking back at the experience, and his performance, fifty years on, Walker observes, "I wish I'd gotten a haircut."[51]

A traveling theater group shows up to entertain. Robert Ball plays the lead mime of this troupe, which both Fonda and Hopper admit was based on a late-1960s Haight-Ashbury group who called themselves The Diggers. Assorted other wives and kids and girlfriends and mistresses of people associated with the production again plumped out the background.

Interestingly, The Diggers had associated with Hopper, and occasionally with Fonda, while in LA. In fact, the actual troupe almost appeared in the film, although apparently, they wanted to be paid more than the film's budget could offer. Diggers member (and future screen actor) Peter Coyote has claimed that the inspiration for *Easy Rider* was actually born out of one of those LA visits in "1968, or early 1969."[52]

Coyote recollects that Fonda, Hopper, and their companion that night, actor Brandon De Wilde, as "our age, sons of the film community, caught somewhere between their home base and their imaginings of free life. Seeking to connect with a pure strain of the underground." According to Coyote, "they picked our brains for stories," including one about, as one member put it, "me and a buddy just riding around, just going around the country, doing what we do, seeing what we see, you know, showing the people what things are like."[53]

Coyote remembers this as the original inspiration for *Easy Rider*. But this is improbable, as *Easy Rider* would begin production on February 23, 1968, around the time this meeting was supposed to have taken place.

Anyway, Wyatt and Billy seem less than impressed with this troupe (not surprisingly, as they are pretty bad), or with the spaced-out audience watching the show. Their attitude reflects yet again how, contrary to what is often assumed, the duo is not of this time, or of this generation, but rather, apparently false outsiders among society's true outsiders.

Fonda seems more sympathetic to this lifestyle choice than his sidekick. For example, when Lisa suggests they give her a ride on their choppers, Hopper objects, only to be reminded by Fonda that "we're eating their food." This line, Hopper generously admitted, was written by Terry Southern, even though at other times, during various mood swings, Hopper has claimed that he wrote the entire script himself.

Hopper also once remarked, and Fonda apparently agreed, that in reality, it was he who was more simpatico to what was going on in society at the time, and that the comparatively less "attuned" Fonda was the one harboring doubt that these lifestyle choices could work out, the flip side of Wyatt and Billy's reactions in the movie itself.

Fonda contracted what turned out to be pneumonia during the commune scenes. Studio ballyhoo later informed the world that this was a result of an allergy to the hay that was used to dress the set, and that had the actor not consulted a doctor when he did, the infection could have been fatal. This may have been more of a publicity stunt than an actual medical opinion, although Fonda did eventually get so sick that he had to be doubled by Kovács during the following (New Mexico–filmed) skinny-dipping scenes, which had to be reshot weeks later when the water, and Fonda, were again available. Hopper tried hard to make sure that these scenes would not be branded as exploitive, a label any other biker movie would have welcomed, by avoiding nudity, and instead going for a more innocent, lyrical quality. "Even simple nudity would have killed the point," he realized.[54] Although here, the lyricism seems more planned than in the Monument Valley scenes. Which was, in fact, the case.

Before they leave the commune, Wyatt and Billy are given a tab of acid by the Stranger, who tells them that "when you get to the right place, with the right people, quarter this," which they do, later on.

Back on the road, Billy and Captain America disrupt a parade by joining in with their choppers and famously "parading without a permit," in scenes shot in Las Vegas, New Mexico, but set in Texas.

Considering that the duo is presumably trying to not attract attention, certainly not the attention of the local police, their interrupting this celebration seems particularly boneheaded. If the script had indicated that this was a protest of some sort—against authority, or the war, or against redneck culture, for example—these actions might conceivably be explainable, if not exactly wise. But Billy and Wyatt never actually get around to demonstrating against anything; as the story continues, they question society (eventually, sort of), but they don't make statements, or stage protests, except inadvertently (through their clothes, for instance), so crashing a small-town parade in this context is meaningless, and not too bright.

Their actions naturally land them in the city jail. These prison interiors were, allegedly, shot in Taos, New Mexico, and they utilized what was still, at the time, that city's actual jail. These jail cells, with their rusted bars and crumbling adobe walls, look frighteningly more like a Hollywood Western movie set than something still being used in the 1960s. Today, the location is still extant, although as Tito's Gallery it now proudly showcases New Mexico artists' overpriced masterworks for tourists rather than local ne'er-do-wells sleeping it off.

Even at the time those cracked walls were covered with graffiti and religious statuary, which Hopper found amusing, or perhaps ironic, and which he readily featured on-camera. To these inadvertent frescos he rather arbitrarily added the names of Foster Denker, a friend who had recently contributed to the biker film *The Angry Breed* (1968), and actor H. D. (Harry Dean) Stanton, another buddy who was already an omnipotent fixture in both low-budget and studio films, and who would continue to appear gloriously in both for the next forty-plus years. (Neither of them, by the way, otherwise contributed anything to *Easy Rider*.)

Another thing this scene gave us was Jack Nicholson. At the time, Nicholson was considering giving up acting. He had been working in Hollywood with no particular distinction since 1956. In 1968 he had just scored relative success as a producer-writer for the Monkees' feature film debut, *Head*. While *Head* itself was not a success, Raybert Productions, which had created the group (and the series, and the movie), had already made a lot of money off of the so-called "pre–Fab Four." Nicholson was considering becoming a full-time producer himself when he came to the attention of acquaintances Fonda and Hopper, through Raybert.

The part of George Hanson was apparently created for Rip Torn, who, unlike the New Jersey–born Nicholson, actually hailed from Texas, and who could have easily projected the gone-to-seed ambiance which the part seemingly called for on the page. There were two problems, however. First off, Torn didn't want to work for scale. Second, he apparently had clashed with Dennis Hopper in a rather dramatic way when in New York in late 1967, Hopper had barged in to a dinner involving Fonda, Torn, Terry Southern, his girlfriend, Gail Gerber, and writer Don Carpenter.

Hopper, who was already wearing his hippie buckskins and handlebar mustache, claimed to have been "scouting locations" in Texas, which was not known as a haven for hippies, and which had apparently lived down to its reputation with Hopper, who became very agitated over Torn's presence at the table. According to Hopper's biographer, Peter L. Winkler, Hopper slurred, "Hey, Rip, you're from fuckin' Texas, aren't you?" Torn admitted that he was, but added, "Don't judge all bastards by me." (Southern was also from Texas, but was disdainful of his good-old-boy roots, and wisely kept his mouth shut.)

When Torn stood up, apparently either to defend himself or his home state, he and Hopper both grabbed butter knives (according to Fonda), or steak knives (according to Torn), and each other's shirts. Author Patrick McGilligan says that Torn then told Hopper, "I'm not going to do your shitty film."[55] The story varies about who threatened who next, and with what, and how far the incident escalated. Eventually Torn left the restaurant, with Hopper (who, according to Winkler, was packing a .45 semiautomatic pistol in his buckskins) threatening to meet Torn outside. Fortunately, this never happened.

Almost thirty years later, in 1994, Dennis Hopper unwisely repeated the story to Jay Leno on *The Tonight Show*, claiming that Torn had first pulled the knife on *him*. Rip Torn subsequently sued Hopper for slander, and in 1996, was awarded $475,000 in damages. Hopper, again unwisely, appealed that judgment, and was subsequently fined an additional $475,000. To this day Rip Torn claims that his career and reputation were damaged by not playing George Hanson.

And they never did film any *Easy Rider* scenes in Texas, either.

Bert Schneider apparently talked Hopper into taking Jack Nicholson, which was fine, as both he and Fonda were already friends with Jack, who would also secretly serve as a spy for Schneider on location, and, as Jack himself later put it, "to stop Dennis and Peter from killing each other."[56]

Nicholson has pretended to be largely ambivalent about the role that would make him a star. In particular, he objected to having to cut his hair to play George Hanson. Future director Henry Jaglom remembers that "We were at Columbia Pictures and I accompanied him down to the barbershop that they used to have. What I remember was [that] in that barbershop—none of us had even been into the barbershop, clearly—were twenty-eight, I counted them, shoes of Jerry Lewis . . . waiting to be cleaned! It was kind of weird. It was this 'other' culture that was using the barbershop."[57]

But Nicholson only acted as if he had just fallen into the role of George Hanson, as if he didn't think he was right for the role, or was indifferent to playing the part—none of which was remotely true. In fact, Jack prepared for the role very carefully. After his haircut, he spent hours rummaging around for Hanson's clothing at Western Costume in Hollywood, finally choosing a seersucker suit, a letter sweater, and, of course, that famous gold football helmet he wears on the back of Captain America's motorcycle, as an external look, and a way inside his character.

George Hanson quickly charms Billy and Wyatt as easily as he does the audience. His sly dialogue, probably courtesy of Southern, is part of it.

"Can you get us off outa here, no sweat?" Billy asks him.

"I imagine that I can, if you haven't killed anybody—least nobody white," he replies.

Southern's biographer, Lee Hill, claims that the author was evoking an oft-used William Faulkner character, Gavin Stevens, although Hopper once, out of nowhere, said that the character was inspired by an actor and future director named Jack Starrett.

The role is pure Jack Nicholson. The "Jack" persona he has cultivated ever since—a smirking, slow-talking, enigmatic, nonconformist—emerges here, fully formed, for the first time. "Here's the making of the star," Fonda joked in a 1995 audio commentary when viewing Nicholson's antics. "He found his voice, and he's been playing George Hanson for twenty films afterwards."[58]

Robert Walker, another friend, agrees. "*Easy Rider* gave Jack the chance to show the world for the first time the wonderful, devilish charm that we all knew that he had. He was driving around town in an old Karmann Ghia then; the convertible top was patched up with duct tape and all tattered. The whole thing was tattered. We were all somewhat tattered. But we were young and trashy and full of beans and mischief. It was a great time."[59]

One of the Nicholson's tics that ever endeared him to audiences was his loopy *nik, nik, nik* sound, which he sputtered every time he took a drink. Nicholson actually appropriated that sound from one of the cycle wranglers, whose name, everyone remembers, was "Gypsy." This Gypsy liked to amuse the crew, and apparently Nicholson, with that sound when he tried to kick-start those bikes. "He was never able to use that thing again after that. People would just think he stole it from Jack," Fonda chuckles.[60]

Gypsy's boss, chief cycle wrangler Tex Hall, had a difficult job on *Easy Rider*. The four Harley-Davidsons were touchy and temperamental, and prone to breaking down. And replacement parts, especially away from the cities in the Heartland, were a virtual impossibility. "You know why they call them Harleys, don't you?" Peter Fonda once asked Roger Corman. "Because they Harley ever start."[61]

Outside the county jail, Hanson admires the boys' bikes, and they invite him along. The song "If You Want to Be a Bird" by the Holy Modal

Rounders plays under the following scene of the trio, with Nicholson, his eyebrows jutting into those familiar inverted V shapes, and a grin seemingly touching both sides of his football helmet, enjoying for the first time the freedom of the open road. It was all a skillful performance, however. The terrified Nicholson reportedly cracked a couple of the chronically unlucky Peter Fonda's ribs while hanging on for dear life with his legs in this scene. The lead vocals for that goofy but memorable song are performed by future playwright-author-actor Sam Shepard!

Again, proving that this movie is seemingly connected to every important event and person of the 1960s, these scenes were allegedly shot on June 5, 1968, the day Robert F. Kennedy was assassinated.

The next campfire scene includes the famous vignette in which Nicholson/Hanson is introduced to marijuana.

"This is the first time that marijuana had ever been smoked in a movie that people who smoked it didn't go out and kill a bunch of nurses or whatever," Hopper once said.[62] It was also, as has often been claimed, the first time in a mainstream movie that real marijuana was used on-screen. Fonda admits that, yes, the reefer was real, but, as noted earlier, not the cocaine. "We couldn't afford it," he says.

Peter Fonda also has said that "there were cops on the set to make sure everything was okay." When this designated representative of authority was on the set, Fonda would have to cryptically state only that he and his costars needed "some more of those hand-rolled cigarettes with the leafy green substance."[63] One has to assume that this clueless policeman was never promoted to detective.

According to Jack Nicholson, 155 joints were smoked on the set of *Easy Rider*. But who, besides, maybe, Jack, was counting?

Hopper's statement about marijuana in the movies, by the way, is not, strictly speaking, true. For example, *International House* (1933) contained the memorable Cab Calloway song "Reefer Man," but didn't feature a single nurse murder. And the (then) much more recent *I Love You, Alice B. Toklas* (1968), a Peter Sellers comedy, included several mayhem-free marijuana references (including, presumably, one in the title). But Hopper has more than occasionally chosen to shore up his shaky arguments without the assistance of any pertinent facts. He also said, for example, that *Pillow Talk*, the famous Rock Hudson–Doris Day hit, had been "made the year we made *Easy Rider*,"[64] presumably to scornfully show how out of touch Hollywood was. The fact that *Pillow Talk* had actually been released ten years earlier, in 1959(!), did not really negate his point, however, because Hollywood *was* out of touch. So, okay, Dennis.

Jack Nicholson recalled that "each time I did a take or angle, it involved smoking almost an entire joint. Now the main portion of this sequence is the transition from not being stoned to being stoned. So after the first take, or two, the main job became reversed. Instead of being straight and having to get stoned in the end, I'm now stoned in the beginning and having to act straight, and then gradually [letting] myself return to where I was—which was very stoned. It was an unusual reversed acting problem," he concluded, perhaps unnecessarily.[65]

In spite of the 155 joints Nicholson ambitiously tabulated, *Easy Rider* remains the rare drug movie which is not really about drugs, just as it towers over all other films as the quintessential biker flick even though it isn't really much concerned with those bikes. Hopper, in fact, has said that "*Easy Rider* was never a motorcycle movie to me. A lot of it was about politically what was going on in the country." Winkler calls this "a strange pronouncement,"[66] presumably because little of a political bent, in either direction, is reflected in the film itself, although Hopper, again, never did seem particularly concerned with this.

Easy Rider, in fact, takes no particular interest in Vietnam, civil rights, campus uprisings, or the assorted assassinations or riots of the era. Its observations are all social, or sociological, rather than political. Which pretty much lines up with what Peter Coyote said about Fonda and Hopper being outside of what was going on in the streets and in the actual counterculture at the time.

In this scene, for example, Nicholson amusingly goes on and on about aliens from Venus secretly integrating themselves into our society. The idea for this dialogue apparently came from Bert Schneider's secretary, who seemed to passionately believe every last breathless word of it. But Nicholson's rambling, pot-infused narrative is just too silly to warrant any alarm, or worry anyone about government cover-ups or conspiracy theories or revolutions, alien or otherwise.

So, *this* revolution, for these narcissistic, self-involved "hippies," really is all about freedom. It's all about personal rather than political freedom, though. It's all about dropping out, and then about getting back out onto that beautiful László Kovács open road. This revolution, for these characters, and for this movie, doesn't concern itself particularly with the "world without" at all, but rather with the world within, and specifically, *their* world within.

The next driving montage includes the semi-immortal "Don't Bogart That Joint" by Fraternity of Man. To "bogart," by the way, is to take an unfair share of something. The move is named after movie great Humphrey Bogart, who presumably "bogarted" cigarettes, not joints. This song segues into Jimi Hendrix's justifiably legendary "If 6 Was 9." Enough said about that.

In the Deep South, the roadside tableaus the trio buzz by become, perhaps only in hindsight, more sinister. Poor people pushing carts and wagons wave at the bikers wearily; in contrast, steel factories belch smoke and white plantations loom upon grassy hillsides.

In Franklin, Louisiana, Kovács's camera grabbed a shot of an upside-down US flag on the side of a storefront. Fonda swears that this was not planned but was a happy accident, and a nice bit of foreshadowing, as an inverted flag is an international symbol of distress.

The famous scene in the diner comes next, shot in Morganza, Louisiana, in June of 1968. The diner was called Melancon's Café, although it was unnamed in the movie, except to very sharp-eyed viewers who might have seen the sign as the choppers pull up in front and park. Melancon's is long gone, sadly, but many residents of Morganza still remember it fondly, along with the day Hollywood rolled into their town.

One of those residents, Donnie "Hair Bear" Derbes, who was thirteen at the time, reminisces:

I lived next door to Melancon's Café, and one day I heard they were going to be filming in there. I didn't know what kind of movie it was going to be, but I did hear that it had motorcycles in it. To a thirteen-year-old, that's plenty of reason to be interested.

Man, when that film crew rode up to that café, the whole town, and people from all over the parish, showed up there just to check them out. They all wanted to see what was going on. So, for a couple of days, our sleepy little town got very busy.

The movie people kept those bikes in a big, white box truck; that's where they worked on them. My friends and I, we were all just in awe of those bikes! So, I went back there and started hanging around with the mechanic that kept the bikes running. His name was Gypsy, and he let me sit on those beautiful bikes when they weren't in use. I thought they were going to fuss at me for sitting on those bikes, but it was just the opposite. They didn't seem to mind. That was the best day of my life.

At first, I kept trying to get into the café to watch the filming. I'd try to sneak in through the back, but was unsuccessful. So, I settled for hanging out with the crew at the truck instead.

I didn't get a chance to meet the stars, but I did once get a little tap on the head from Dennis Hopper; it was kinda like a "hey, little man" sort of tap.[67]

To secure Melancon's for the shoot, the filmmakers followed their usual operating procedure of sending out a straight-looking representative (usually Paul Lewis) in a conservative-looking suit and tie to arrange the location. Every town seemed to have a little theater group that would offer to donate their valuable talents to the production. They only "wanted to know if it was a real Hollywood film," Fonda remembers, "and if [their] mother would be able to watch it. Of course, we said yes to everything."[68]

Hopper, however, did not want these "actors." He wanted actual, and actually belligerent, locals. When the scruffy crew finally entered Melancon's Café, the theater group was waiting for them on one side of the diner, and the real customers were on the other.

"I want those guys over there," Hopper said, pointing to the very hostile-looking locals, including the local deputy sheriff (Arnold Hess Jr.), also quite antagonistic. Hopper then proceeded to stoke the fires by telling those angry diners that their characters had just raped and killed a young girl out of town, which amped up the tension even further.

Dennis Hopper also found some gawking female teenagers in a booth and asked them to feign interest in the trio. He sat with them for twenty minutes, as Fonda recalls, trying to describe to the girls what he wanted from them. Finally, one of the teens said, "You mean, all you want us to do is *flirt* with you? Oh, we know how to do that."[69]

Hopper instructed the girls to do "that" without telling the other locals about it, making the malice in the room even more palpable. The comments by the increasingly agitated locals, along the lines of "They look like a bunch of refugees from a gorilla love-in," could probably never have been scripted, even by Terry Southern.

Unfortunately, the scene doesn't lead to any sort of a climax. Not here. Although the ominous and prophetic words "I don't think they'll make the parish line" provide some creepy foreshadowing. The scene ends with the bikers understandably beating a nervous retreat. According to Hopper, the sequence was originally twenty minutes longer, although it always ended the same way—with the guys being followed out to their choppers by the smitten high schoolers, and being watched with increasing unease by the deputy sheriff and his toadies.

The ever-unlucky Fonda blew out his right ankle trying to kick-start his bike when these scenes were shot. He had to have his boot cut away at the hotel that night due to swelling. Hopper also had to cut away to the staring rednecks to hide the accident. In the next scene Fonda was forced to keep his swollen foot hidden.

That next scene was yet another campfire sequence. The script has already established that the trio is not welcome at any respectable hotel (although this is mentioned, redundantly, in the following dialogue anyway), but these scenes do harken back, again, to Hollywood Westerns, which, again, proved a bigger influence, and inspiration, to the story than would be commented upon at the time.

This is also the scene when Nicholson gets to voice many of the film's big ideas, or at least, what people at the time thought were its big ideas.

"You know, this used to be a hell of a good country. I can't understand what's gone wrong with it," he says.

Hopper takes a drag and says about the people of that country that "they think we're going to cut their throat or something . . . they're scared," which is ironic, since in the previous scene, Hopper as a director had stirred up these same fears among the extras in the diner.

Hanson: "Oh, they're not afraid of you. They're afraid of what you represent."

Billy: "Hey, man, all we represent to them is someone who needs a haircut."

Hanson: ". . . What you represent to them is freedom."

Billy: "What the hell's wrong with freedom, man—that's what it's all about."

Hanson: "Oh yeah, that's right, that's what it's all about. But talkin' about it and being it, that's two different things. I mean, it's real hard to be free when you're bought and sold in the marketplace. But don't ever tell anybody that they're not free, because then they're going to get real busy killin' and maiming to prove to you that they are. Oh yeah, they're going to talk to you, and talk to you, and talk to you about individual freedom. But they see a free individual, it's gonna scare 'em."

This dialogue seems to sum up why this "good country" is apparently now rotting at the core. But this same type of situation, without the marijuana and the sixties slang, had been appearing in Westerns for many years. The theme of the cowboy—a free man, who is resented, or envied, or destroyed for it—shows up time and time again, going back to James Fenimore Cooper. *Young Mr. Lincoln* (1939) and *The Ox-Bow Incident* (1943), for example, both starred Henry Fonda and dealt with violence against outsiders on the frontier. Another Fonda movie, *The Grapes of Wrath* (1940), also dealt with drifters, in this case displaced Dust Bowl farmers, who also meet with prejudice and violence on Route 66 while crossing the country.

John Wayne, who would costar with Hopper in *True Grit*, also released in 1969, specialized in playing the anachronistic cowboy, the tough old son-of-a-bitch who had tamed the West to make it safe for civilization, although that civilization then had no place for his freedom-loving ways, a theme which surfaces constantly throughout Wayne's films.

In the 1950s and '60s, many "modern" Westerns were produced bemoaning a world where there was no room for the cowboy, examples of which could include *Giant* (1956), *The Misfits* (1960), *Lonely Are the Brave* (1962), and *Hud* (1963). There was also a lighter, more-comedic take on the same theme in *The Rounders* (1965), another Henry Fonda Western that Peter, in particular, might have been familiar with.

At the time, Peter Fonda was not consciously trying to evoke either specific Hollywood Westerns, or his father, or his father's on-screen persona. Yet, as Patrick McGilligan noticed, "With hindsight it occurred to Fonda that George Hanson, not Captain America—Jack Nicholson, not Peter Fonda—was the one doing the Henry Fonda impression. Nicholson was the one playing the pure American."

"He really is a patriot. He reads that line . . . with the authority that only comes if you believe in it. . . . [H]e read it like Henry. He's the Tom Joad, in a way, of our era," Fonda said in one interview, referring to the seminal part his father had played in John Ford's production of Steinbeck's *Grapes of Wrath*.[70]

One should not take Fonda's Captain America persona at face value anyway. The character is not so Christ-like as he would appear, which Fonda was doubtless aware of, as was Hopper. In 1969 Dennis Hopper told *Evergreen* magazine that the Wyatt character represented "the great white liberal who keeps saying everything's going to work out, but doesn't do anything to help it work out. . . . Does he break the $50,000 out of the gas tank? What does he do? Nothing?"[71]

That night, much like in *The Ox-Bow Incident*, the party is attacked, presumably by the locals from the diner, and George Hanson is killed. The scene is dramatically shot by Hopper, but it feels incomplete, as if none of the principals were on the set that night, although you do, briefly see the yellow "Cat" baseball cap one of the more-sinister townspeople had been wearing earlier.

The sequence includes a lot of close-ups of sticks swinging and people grimacing, and the soundtrack is full of crickets chirping and dogs barking and people screaming, but it feels incomplete. Perhaps this is because it's hard to figure out why the townspeople would have left Billy and Wyatt alive as witnesses—although Hopper later implied that Hanson had to die because he was one of "them" and a traitor to "straight" America, and that the others were spared as a warning to other outsiders to keep away. He does not elaborate upon how the locals would have known this about George Hanson, however.

Fonda, at least, was more specific. In 1970 he said that "we felt Jack's character had to die because he was the innocent: The only reason he got destroyed is because he was with us. If he'd gone through town on his own, they wouldn't have touched him. That's the message I wanted to put down there."[72] In 2002 Peter Fonda further elaborated on this by explaining that "[Hanson's] innocent. He's got to die in any good Greek mythological comedy or tragedy; innocence is the first thing that gets lopped."[73]

The scene also lacks payoff. It removes George Hanson from the plot after only twenty minutes, and it steers Wyatt and Billy to the New Orleans whorehouse as a tribute to their martyred friend. But one has to wonder: Did they just leave that friend's bloody body behind at the campsite? They do mention that they need to send his belongings home, but do they ever do so? Also, in spite of the wounds which seemingly had been inflicted upon them during that attack, the next time we see them, Wyatt and Billy seem to be largely okay, except for some minor abrasions on their faces that vary a bit in color and size between shots. In fact, they are having dinner in a fancy restaurant, which apparently is also "with it" enough to serve "their kind." The Electric Prunes somewhat eerily perform the liturgy "Kyrie Eleison" under this scene.

In reality, this restaurant was called Rob Roy's, and according to Fonda, it was not in New Orleans but on Wilshire Boulevard in Los Angeles. The next location, "Madam Tinkertoy's House of Blue Lights," was also filmed in LA, actually at the private home of either an "actress," as Fonda remembers, or a "decorator," according to Hopper. The two do agree that it was somewhere in the Los Feliz district, east of Hollywood, and that the residence was empty at the time and so had to be "dressed" for the shoot. No one from the studio remembered to bring prop books for the library, however, so the bookcases there, just like the rest of the whorehouse itself, is curiously empty. (So where *are* all the horny "johns" who must be in town for Mardi Gras?) Presumably reading would not have been a priority at Madam Tinkertoy's anyway.

Lea Marmer presumably plays the role of Madam Tinkertoy, although she is billed only as "Madam." Marmer was, like Nicholson, another Raybert carryover, having appeared several times in *The Monkees*. Her girls, as noted, are played by Karen Black, as Karen, and Toni Basil as Mary.

"I suggested Karen [for] that job," Henry Jaglom asserts. "She was my girlfriend at the time, and I had a feeling she would be great. The rest is history."[74] In 1968, however, Black was somewhat adrift in that she professed little experience with narcotics, which made her a bit of an anomaly on the set. Likewise, Basil knew Hopper, slightly, as they were both acquaintances of experimental artist and filmmaker Bruce Conner. Basil and Black were returnees from the earlier, and very chaotic, New Orleans location shoot.

A failing of *Easy Rider*, certainly to modern audiences, is its characterization of women. All of the women in the film are presented as straights, hippies, groupies, or hookers, and they all act precisely the same way. Throughout the movie, men suggest to the ladies that they alternately plant crops, drop acid, or go skinny-dipping, and the women immediately fall compliantly into line to do so.

Fonda had not wanted Captain America to go to a whorehouse. The plot contrivance of going as a tribute to Hanson does get the duo inside, but once there, the four of them had to quickly get out onto the street so that the Mardi Gras footage Hopper and company had taken earlier could be utilized. Even allowing for the clunky mechanics of the plotting here, the girls without hesitation simply march with these two oddly dressed and not exactly affluent-looking freaks, right out into the chaos. Are the ladies even slightly worried about their personal safety? Did they get paid first? Hell, do they *ever* get paid? And do they ever wonder for a second about the wisdom of taking mysterious drugs on the street—during Mardi Gras, yet—with these two? Is this little field trip something Karen and Mary *want* to do, or do they tag along because they have been told to do so by their madam, or their johns? Even allowing that this is the 1960s, it's interesting that none of this is addressed. The movie just doesn't seem very interested in the girls as anything other than pretty props.

What follows is the most experimental part of a movie, which, as has been discussed, has a reputation for being more experimental than it actually is. As much as Fonda and Hopper might have wanted to escape from the yoke of studio filmmaking, they were both basically baby boomers, suckled on narrative Hollywood cinema. Peter Fonda had literally grown up around the movies, and Dennis Hopper had done so by first watching the movies, and later, acting in them, having appeared in Hollywood films for more than ten years by this point. So, their influences would have been, to a large degree, conventional narrative cinema, perhaps in spite of themselves. *Easy Rider*'s numerous echoes of Hollywood Westerns and road movies certainly bear this out. But Hopper also wanted to do something experimental, something European here, and he did. Whether this experiment worked to the benefit of the rest of his film is, well, debatable.

The first problem is the 16mm format itself. This footage looks markedly different from the rest of the movie, especially considering how magnificent and beautiful the Kovács footage surrounding it is. The smaller image size and additional grain *could* represent the effects of the characters' acid trip, but if so, then why does all of the footage taken here—not just the point-of-view and post-acid shots—look this way?

Hopper does use a lot of lens flares here, at the time a new and even controversial effect, and something which Kovács mimics, to better effect, in his footage. One take Hopper was considerably pleased with has his camera tilting up along a mausoleum row into the sunshine. "When you get to the top, you see the energy of the sun like a flame thrower coming through to blank out the screen. It was an amazing shot," he remembered proudly.[75] And yes, that particular strip of film is kind of cool to look at.

Hopper was probably influenced by the recent success of *2001: A Space Odyssey* (1968), which concluded with a psychedelic light show that was dazzling straights and stoners alike in theaters while *Easy Rider* was in gestation. Publicity for that film called it the "ultimate trip." Hopper's sequence is a trip as well. He throws so much into it that it certainly could be called audacious, if not particularly coherent.

All kinds of things occur. In a cemetery the four of them take communion, which consists of dropping the acid tab from the commune (apparently Mary and Karen were the prophesied "right people"). Mary disrobes between two vaults. Karen dances about amid the graves. Karen also free-associates about how she could not "feel inside" her body. (Basil, her roommate during the New Orleans shoot, talked Black into using this dialogue after she mentioned a dream/experience she had had which included those symptoms.) Meanwhile, Billy tosses a cross about and disrupts a funeral service, or perhaps imagines he has. He also, briefly, seems to be raping Karen. About this time, a man in a black suit with an umbrella dances through the scene in what is apparently Hopper's Jean Cocteau homage. All the while, scripture and weeping and heavy machinery pile-drive on the soundtrack.

It is Captain America, or perhaps Fonda himself, who is most exposed in this confounding sequence. Hopper somehow persuaded his costar to climb onto a statue of a woman in the cemetery and talk to it as if it were his mother. A sensitive topic, because Fonda's mother had committed suicide when Peter was ten. "Why did you leave like that?" Fonda sobs. His emotion is so real and so raw here that the sequence briefly transcends the gimmickry around it and becomes almost embarrassingly intimate. Although probably accidental, this little revelation, if one cares to consider it, explains some of Wyatt's character quirks—his aloofness, his "incompleteness," and even his ability, as someone who has already seen into the abyss, to comprehend his ultimate failure, and that of his generation.

Abruptly, and with no mention of whatever befell Mary or Karen, the film then returns Billy and Wyatt to 35mm, and to the open road. Considering what has happened, and what is about to happen, the scenery that they are shown blowing past should perhaps be even more foreshadowingly sinister than it is, or than the earlier, and similar, Deep South footage was, but there is still something very much off here. Industrial wastelands and factories are again juxtaposed with tree-lined mansions; the girders on the bridges they pass now look like prison bars, the rusting industrial equipment, like skeletons. The two bikes keep weaving in front of and behind one another in this scene; they never seem to be on the same plane at the same time. "We're going forward, but we're not progressing,"[76] Hopper commented, anticipating, maybe, again, what is coming. "Flash, Bam, Pow" by The Electric Flag accompanies the scene.

Another campfire scene, the film's last, follows. This sequence was shot after the rest of the movie had wrapped. In fact, it wasn't until after the wrap party that ever-attentive producer Fonda remembered that they had forgotten to shoot that last campfire scene.

But there was a problem. The bikes were already gone. One, or maybe both, of them had been completely destroyed for the climax. The other two had been stolen from Tex Hall's garage in Simi Valley, where they were being stored.

There has been a lot of speculation as to who took those bikes, because of their value after the fact. But as the movie had not come out yet, was not even finished yet when the theft occurred, it is not likely the bikes were stolen by collectors. Some romantic speculation has indicated that the Hells Angels took the choppers in retribution against Peter Fonda, for his treatment of their club in *The Wild Angels* (1966), although since whatever bad-blood-causing incident had happened on that set had occurred almost three years earlier, it's difficult to speculate how the Angels could have connected these bikes to Fonda. So, if this is true, then the Angels need to be complimented both on their patience and their very keen deductive skills.

It's much more likely that the choppers were stolen to be chopped up for parts. Peter Fonda was again quoted as saying, this time in the Guggenheim Museum's "Art of the Motorcycle" exhibit catalog in 1998, that "I like the idea that in a variety of places around the country, folks are riding parts of those bikes. Underneath some metal-flake-painted tank somewhere, there are [the] Stars and Stripes. And the owner doesn't have a clue."[77]

Actually, Tex Hall, according to Fonda, claimed to have known who took the bikes. Fonda has also said that he "heard" that "Tex went after their house with a machine gun and shot the place up pretty good."[78] This is a dramatic-sounding anecdote, to be sure, but with only Fonda's hazy third-person memories to go on, sadly impossible to substantiate after all these years.

And so, for only the second time in all of this film's many campfire scenes, we just see Wyatt and Billy in front of that flickering fire, no bikes, no George Hanson, no hitchhikers. Once again, the Santa

Monica Mountains stood in for more-distant locations here. The scene, minimalist as it is, remains one of the most-enigmatic and oft-discussed sequences in cinema.

Hopper and Fonda had always intended to have a segment in which the two outlaws discuss the "theme" of the picture, whatever it was. But on the set, Fonda refused to say any of the paragraphs of dialogue Hopper intended to use. Instead, he just wanted Captain America to say only "We blew it," knowing that the audience would wonder, perhaps for the rest of their lives, what exactly "it" was. To this day, Fonda, like Captain America, is coy about what the statement was actually referring to, or even what he *thought* the statement referred to. In a 1970 *Playboy* interview, however, he did offer these thoughts:

> *Literally within the story, we blew it when we went for the easy money and then thought we could retire. And we thought that was the basis of freedom. Look, there are two parts to the American dream: The first is, get it all together no matter who goes down. The no-matter-who-goes-down idea isn't spoken too loudly, sometimes not at all, but it's there. The second part is: And then retire. To me, both of those are untenable positions. I can't in all good conscience get it all together no matter who goes down, nor can I retire. In a broader sense, we blew it because liberty is just a statue in New York Harbor—a polluted harbor. We've blown it because we've spent so much money on so many insane endeavors—germ warfare, ABM [antiballistic missiles], MIRV [multiple independently targetable reentry vehicles], Vietnam, Cambodia. We've blown our freedom in the books we don't read and in the universities that don't teach. We've blown it around the world—and not just Americans. Everybody's blown it. We've gotten it together only on an economic level and only in some parts of the world, and not for any other reason. Well, I promise you that when you base your life solely on economics—as Wyatt and Billy did in* Easy Rider—*you blow your life right out the window.*[79]

Amusingly, Fonda also carps that Hopper has repeatedly said that "Peter never understood why I made him say the line."

"I would like to make it clear that at no time did I not understand why I said that line. I *wrote* that line!" Fonda has angrily asserted.[80]

Dennis Hopper, for his part, never hesitated during the following decades to give his opinion about what he, and this scene, and this movie, were really trying to say. Unfortunately, that opinion has changed repeatedly over the years, depending on the actor's mood, or his audience, or his preferred stimulant at that moment. Although, to be fair, he did seem to be trying to make the same point, just at different times and with different words.

A few of Hopper's "We blew it" explanations:

- "'We blew it' meant to me that they could have spent that energy on something other than smuggling cocaine, could have done something other than help society destroy itself" (1969).[81]

- "We blew it because we three [*sic*] colorful character were *criminals*. We smuggled drugs, we used amoral ways to buy our way out of the system. That's why we blew it" (1987).[82]

- "The motorcycles, those beautiful machines in the movie, really represent the American creation. But the two riders skimming across the country don't know what they're doing. They've blown it. Really copped out" (1988).[83]

- "I thought the big chrome machine with [the] Stars and Stripes on it would blow up and destroy itself. We've blown it. We've blown what? We've blown our heritage by not being responsible for being free" (1995).[84]

- "We blew whatever chance we had to be something good. Something inspired, something different" (1999).[85]

- "The two outlaws who've gone for the big money, and gotten rich, the American dream. In point of fact they've undermined their country and are destroying it. And that was the story to me. They've lost sight of their freedom" (2009).[86]

Over the years, many others who were less close to the material have grappled with the concept as well. In 2009, *Mojo* magazine music journalist Michael Simmons said, "It is *the* film of its time. It defines the 1960s. Including the ending. Most amazingly, it got it! That ending understood that there was something flawed at the heart of the counterculture. Wyatt represented us . . . Fonda's enigmatic line at the end, 'We blew it,' it indicates that we all blew it . . . You have to figure it out for yourself. It's one of the beauties of the line—that it forces the audience to think."[87]

And then, in the very next scene, it all ends. On the road, specifically Highway 105 outside Krotz Springs, Louisiana, the two of them are passed by a couple of rednecks in a pickup truck. They brandish a rifle to try to scare Billy, who, Billy-like to the end, instead flips them off. So, those two locals—played by two locals, Johnny David and David C. Billodeau—proceed to just . . . shoot him.

Captain America comes back for his friend, covers him with his flag jacket, and gets back on his bike to go for help. But the truck returns and Wyatt is shot too. His bike rolls off the road and the gas tank full of cash explodes.

So did the audience.

"The people did not know how to react. They had never seen a movie like that in their lives," Fonda has said.[88]

Karen Black agreed. "When you left that film, when you left the theater, you didn't leave; you were still fighting it, fighting the ending, trying to change the ending."[89]

A more-reflective Michael Simmons, with the benefit of hindsight, has said that "I was moved by the ending, on a dramatic level, but as a hippie I was a little disappointed with it, because as a hippie I thought it was saying 'Everything you believe in is going to turn to shit.' Well, everything we did believe in did turn to shit."

The ending of the film has fired almost as much discussion as the "We blew it" scene. Once again, Hopper offered the most surprising interpretation, to Tom Burke of the *New York Times*, in 1969:

> *Everybody seems confused about the end of this picture, and all I'm saying is that we aren't very different [from] the two guys in the truck who shot us. That all of us, man, are herd-instincted animals. That we all need each other. And why can't the different herds mingle?*

What I want to say with Easy Rider *is: Don't be scared; go and try to change America, but if you're gonna wear a badge, whether it's long hair or black skin, learn to protect yourselves. Go in groups, but go. When people understand that they can't tramp on you, maybe they'll start accepting you. Accepting* all *herds.*[90]

The filmmakers wanted Bob Dylan's "It's Alright, Ma" (also known as "It's Only Bleeding") for the soundtrack here. Dylan, when asked whether they could use the song, requested to see the movie, so Fonda and Hopper invited him to a screening at Columbia's offices in New York.

"Why did you kill those guys at the end?" the musician asked Hopper angrily after the lights came up. "Why doesn't Peter come back and blow those guys away in the pickup truck?"

Fonda told him, "Oh, you want some revenge, Bob. Well, that's the whole idea; we're not letting anybody have any revenge. You have to truck this out of the movie house and take it home with you and live with it and try to figure it out."[91]

Although Dylan did seem to want to *talk* about *Easy Rider*, he didn't seem to want his song to appear on the film's soundtrack. He complained that he was unhappy with the lyrics he'd written, and that he didn't like his harmonica solo. Exasperated, Fonda told him that *he* hated, and was embarrassed by, the scene where he talked to the cemetery statue as if it were his mother, but that it was there in the movie for him to live with. So be it.

It was eventually agreed that Roger McGuinn would perform Dylan's song in the movie. Dylan then grabbed a cocktail napkin and started to write out some entirely new lyrics. "Give this to McGuinn," he said. "He'll know what to put to it."

McGuinn (from The Byrds, who had already contributed "I Wasn't Born to Follow") took Dylan's scribbled lyrics and added some of his own. Significantly, he also added the phrase "All they wanted, was to be free, and that's the way it turned out to be," which Fonda, in particular, absolutely loved.

McGuinn's subsequent song, now called "The Ballad of *Easy Rider*," became a major hit, although Bob Dylan took no credit, and only recently has Fonda acknowledged the nature of his participation.

Dylan, by the way, spent much of 1969 *not* appearing on the soundtracks of hit movies. He wrote the successful "Lay Lady Lay" for that year's *Midnight Cowboy*, but did not finish the lyrics in time for the song to be included in the film.

Easy Rider famously ends with a helicopter shot of Wyatt's burning bike in the grass, and of a river running parallel to the carnage. Fonda told Dylan that the shot represented the two roads—the road of man, and the road of nature.

By the time they were ready to get that shot, in yet another horrible sign of the times, Bobby Kennedy had been assassinated, and the government, fearing further violence, had suspended private aviation rentals. When László Kovács finally found a pilot willing to take him up, he had to quickly jury-rig a camera car mount, counterbalanced with sandbags, outside the door of the little chopper, which the pilot told him was now too heavy to fly. "This helicopter has a smaller engine than your Mustang," he told the uneasy Kovács.[92]

Ultimately, it did take several tries for the helicopter to be able to pull up high enough, and at the right angle, to get the shot that Hopper envisioned. This was terrifying for Kovács, who had to straddle the equipment and operate the camera from outside the open doorway.

The pilot of that helicopter was one Barry Seal, who would later be involved in a drug deal that would lead to his subsequent murder. In the TV movie *Doublecrossed* (1991) that told his story, Seal would be played by Dennis Hopper.

CHAPTER THREE

Movies Are Random!

PETER FONDA AND DENNIS HOPPER RETURNED TO CALIFORNIA, THIS time most definitely *not* via motorcycle. The film had been shipped home to Hollywood, as it was being exposed on the road, so Schneider and Rafelson knew what Kovács seeking camera had captured, but Fonda and Hopper did not. Once Hopper showed up, he insisted that he be allowed to edit the film himself, although Rayburn assigned him a professional cutter, Donn Cambern, as well. Cambern had first met with Hopper on the Madam Tinkertoy's House of Blue Lights set in Los Feliz, and Hopper, although obviously distracted, nonetheless had hired Cambern on the spot. So, now there were countless miles of film, shot on countless miles of open road, for the two of them to screen together and ponder and edit and score.

Cambern recalls that "Looking at the dailies, you could tell that there was a vision. I thought already that there was something special about this movie. And by the time Dennis came back from the road, I had already put together a lot of the film—but there was a lot left to do. Dennis wanted everything that he had shot in, no matter what it was."[93]

One of Hopper's main tenets in editing was to use direct cuts only, as opposed to dissolves or fades, which most Hollywood movies relied upon, but which European cinema seldom utilized. Hopper did not know at the time that this was chiefly because it was more expensive to pay the lab to dissolve from one scene to another than to direct-cut. Even when he did figure this out, he continued to utilize direct cutting only, thinking it would improve his chances of winning the Cannes Film Festival—his dream—where he still believed that "superimposes were frowned upon."[94]

Hopper, in fact, wanted to go *beyond* what was being done in movies made across the Atlantic. Fonda remembers him shouting "Fuck those Europeans, man, they ain't *never* going to see a movie like this. We're going to have jump cuts going from left to right, right to left, up and down, in and out—they're gonna wonder what the hell's happening."[95]

The truth is, although the film does contain few fades or dissolves, a more-interesting transitional approach was created by Cambern. This technique was first utilized some eleven minutes into the film when Billy and Captain America's first campfire scene is interrupted by several lightning-quick flash cuts of the abandoned barn to be seen *in the next scene*. The effect is audacious and experimental, but as Cambern realized—and Hopper probably didn't—it was too distracting, too much of a "What the hell is happening" moment to use too often after that.

The director liked to say that he spent a year sleeping on the floor of a pool house while cutting his 127,000 feet of film (Fonda claims it was "only" twenty-two weeks). Cambern disputes all of this. "Jesus Christ, I don't recall any pool house, ever! We started cutting first in an office on Highland Avenue. It was a small dubbing and editing facility. Dennis and I were there alone. We had ten weeks to get his cut ready, but we weren't even getting close. Bert Schneider called, and he said, 'I want you to move over to Columbia Pictures'—which we did. Raybert was in a two-story office on the lot, two big editing rooms. I had an assistant, and then another assistant came in as well."[96]

Hopper was offered a role in *True Grit* during this period and turned it down, only to have Schneider force him into accepting by promising "not to touch the movie while you're gone."[97] When Hopper got back from location in Colorado (which had been improbably cast as Oklahoma for the film), tanned, but anxious, he dutifully went back to work with Cambern.

Hopper finally emerged from the cutting room dragging behind him what has been reported as an up to four-and-a-half-hour *Easy Rider*. Cambern remembers it as four hours and thirteen minutes. Fonda recalls that Hopper did eventually get it down to two hours and forty-five minutes, with a "scene missing" notification where the diner scene needed to go, which meant the complete film would have been three hours long at that point. Those who saw this cut with its variant and contested running times remember that scenes of the guys on their bikes would go on for entire reels, or so it seemed. That diner sequence alone, in the eventual Hopper cut, ran for more than twenty minutes (for reference, in the version we have today, this scene is a brisk three and a half minutes).

Hopper's inspiration was again, *2001: A Space Odyssey* (1968), which like other event movies of the era had been "road-showed," meaning that it would run on a reserved-seat basis with an intermission. Hopper blatantly admitted this influence in a 1969 interview, where, significantly, he remarked on his attempt to "get the real feeling for the ride, very hypnotic, very beautiful, like in *2001*."[98] Of course, Hopper wanted *Easy Rider* to get the same treatment. Bill Hayward told him that "Columbia isn't going to do that, Dennis. There's no chance in the world that they're going to road-show this movie."[99]

The problem was that Hopper *liked* the film the way it was, and didn't want to touch a frame. "Some French director saw it and told him not to cut it," Henry Jaglom remembers—advice which Hopper was very much determined to follow. Cambern recalls that even in the long version, the film was "already in there, but you still had to dig for it."[100] The key was getting Hopper to let someone else do that digging.

Henry Jaglom, who was working in the Raybert offices at the time, was one of those who saw Hopper's version. He remembers that "for reasons I still don't understand, I was the only one who wasn't stoned at that particular screening, so for me it was a little boring. The others in the audience loved it because each ride went on for twenty, twenty-five minutes, with two, three, or four songs going, and I got a little restless because I wasn't high, and I was working on real time."[101]

The ever-democratic Schneider then told Cambern, Henry Jaglom, Peter Fonda, and Jack Nicholson that "You're all involved in this; if you have something that you want to contribute, look at it with Donn." Cambern recalls that "we would run the footage, Burt, Dennis, Jack, Henry, myself, and then we would go to Bert's abode on Friday nights and smoke joints and talk about the film until God knows how late. I lasted about two weeks! I said to Bert, 'I've got a family, and kids; you guys go ahead. You can then tell me all about it on Monday morning.'"[102]

Henry Jaglom was involved because, believe it or not, Bert Schneider had once been Jaglom's summer camp counselor at Kamp Kohut in Oxford, Maine. In 1969, Jaglom was an aspiring actor, and through Schneider and Rafelson, had been cast opposite Sally Field in both *Gidget* (1965–1966) and *The Flying Nun* (1967–1970) at Columbia Pictures. He had also shot footage in 1967 of the Six-Day War in Israel, on 8mm, which he had subsequently shown to Schneider.

"I had to edit this stuff in the camera," Jaglom said. "I didn't know anything about editing. I didn't even know that you could splice or move the footage around after you had shot it. But Bert must have thought I did, because I had bored him with that silent Six-Day War footage the year before. So, he gave me the film, myself and Jack Nicholson, because we had both decided that we wanted to direct. We had adjacent editing rooms. We started on opposite sides of the movie and agreed to meet in the middle, Jack said, 'Do me a favor and cut my stuff; I don't want to be accused of self-aggrandizement.' When I got to Jack's scenes, though, I had to keep cutting to highlight him anyway, because he was so good."[103]

Cambern agrees with Jaglom's memories of this period—to a point.

"I took suggestions from Henry and Jack," Cambern recalls. "Sometimes they were good suggestions; many times, they were terrible. But, without question I was the editor, and without question, I did all of the work. I looked at it. I cut every single frame. The result was this wonderful, marvelous picture. I think my contribution was a major one."[104]

For his part, Henry Jaglom stresses that he and Nicholson were supervised by Rafelson and by Schneider, and by Cambern, who taught them the mechanics and rhythms of the craft. As Jaglom learned that craft, he quickly noticed (and was surprised by) how often it benefited the film to favor Fonda in the editing room. "Compared to Dennis's spaciness and his penchant for saying 'man' in every sentence, and to Jack's volatility and emerging star quality, Peter was the only one up there that we didn't have to keep chipping away at in the editing room. His performance, his presence on-screen, is the central force, the true and silent center of *Easy Rider*. Peter has, in my opinion, never gotten enough credit for that performance. It's very difficult to play stoic; it's hard to play enigmatic. At his best, Fonda here evokes the same bedrock qualities his father had. It's a shame he hasn't played to those strengths in his persona very often since then; probably, I guess, because he doesn't wish to evoke those comparisons.[105]

"I did make one big mistake," Jaglom continues.

So, Bert said, "I'll pay you $1,000 a week, or you can take half a point profit participation." I went to my dad for advice. He was a very wise man. He explained to me how the movies are so random, how they seldom ever go into profit, and that I should take the money up front. Thanks, Dad!

I'll always remember that there was some secretary or someone in the office who was offered the same deal as me, and she took the point! She eventually made something like $65,000. I don't know if that's the actual number, but I do remember it was some staggeringly enormous amount. The funny thing was, afterwards my father still insisted to me that I had done the right thing, because, as he said, movies are random. And ultimately, because of what happened, Bert told me that he would instead give Jack and I each an opportunity to direct. And he did. I directed A Safe Place *(1971), which Jack appeared in, and Jack directed* Drive, He Said *(1971), which I appeared in. Yes, movies are random!*[106]

Donn Cambern was apparently better attuned to the film's commercial prospects than Henry Jaglom's dad.

At one point I asked Bert to come in and I said, "You know, I'd like very much to buy a piece of this film, just one point." The budget was only $350,000, and that was primarily Bert's money. I said, "You know, I can give you $5,000 for a point." And he said, "Well, Donn, I gotta think about it." He came back a couple days later, [and] said, "No, Donn; we've come this far. We're going to stay with it." But he ended up giving me a smaller piece, after the picture was finished, anyway. That sent both of my sons to college. I owe quite a debt, in that sense, to Easy Rider!*[107]

By the way, the $350,000 budget Cambern mentions is the equivalent of about $2.5 million today. Cambern also calculates that Bert Schneider's ultimate piece of the movie could have netted the producer, by his estimate, over $30 million!

Near the end of the process, Cambern, frustrated, again called Schneider. "I said, 'I can't get anything done. These guys are just switching egos back and forth; everybody wants to try something. We have a good movie here. I know we can pull it out. We're getting so close. I just need to sit down, alone, with you.' So, Bert turned to Dennis, to Peter, to Jack, to Henry, and he just said, 'Okay, I want you all to leave now.'"[108]

Henry Jaglom disputes this. "Believe me, I'd remember if anything like that had taken place. I don't want to diminish Cambern's earlier contribution. He was a perfectly good conventional editor, but as I remember it, the film was a little much for him, very special and weird and unconventional; that's what made it so successful. I mean, Cambern was a nice, regular guy and we were all these weird creative artists, these '60s freaks, Jack and Bob and I, we all were directors-to-be, so it's a little odd and unreal for you to have an editor claim that at the end, Bert 'sent us all away' so that he could 'finish things up.' Bert never 'sent us away' until the final cut was made."[109]

Schneider also had trouble, predictably, with Dennis. He made this trouble go away by making the director go away. He offered two tickets, for Hopper and his new girlfriend, to Taos, New Mexico, both of which Hopper had recently fallen in love with, to get him out of the cutting room.

By this time the film that Schneider and Cambern were watching in that cutting room was only "ten to twenty minutes over its final length, and it was really starting to show us how good it could be. Bert would look at a reel, make suggestions, I'd make suggestions," Cambern recalls. "Left alone, within two weeks we had the cut."[110]

The ninety-five-minute version that Cambern claims he and Schneider eventually hacked out of Hopper's supersized *Easy Rider* was everything the studio wanted, assuming that they had wanted a biker film at all. This *Easy Rider* was tight, lean, and focused; it was viable, and commercial. Although many of Hopper's stylistic "European" flourishes and transitional direct cuts were still there, they were now in a format more digestible to Americans.

In spite of rampant rumors among *Easy Rider* fans, only two major scenes were cut entirely out of the finished film. One of them involved Captain America and Billy after the cocaine deal has gone down, being followed by the police and having to hide in the bushes from helicopters to get away. The other discarded sequence involved the duo getting into a big fight at a roadhouse and subsequently being thrown out. "Both of those sequences did nothing for the film," Cambern recalls. "I remember Bert saying, 'Let's get these out—this is terrible.'"[111]

Incidentally, Columbia Pictures acquired all of the film's outtakes and discarded footage in 1997, which they have since been unable to locate. Fonda, aware that the studio owns the finished film only, thinks the outtakes were destroyed intentionally, so any fans' dreams of ever seeing the "complete" *Easy Rider* will probably never be realized. Although, you just never know. "A big enough gun, I bet I could find the sucker. Maybe I should offer a reward—a million dollars to the person who finds the outtakes for *Easy Rider*," Peter Fonda joked (maybe it was a joke) in 2011.[112]

Not surprisingly, everyone was happier with this new *Easy Rider*. And also not surprisingly, no one wanted to show it to its director.

"I'm one of those directors who happens to think a director isn't a director unless he does every little bit of his own editing," Hopper had said, so no one wanted to be in the room when the new version was introduced to its creator.[113]

This ultimately took place "at Columbia, in the big theater," Bill Hayward recalled. "And I just thought, he's going to go so nuts when he sees what we've done. He's my brother-in-law and I liked him, but he had a temper. I knew this was cutting into his creative soul. . . . I was prepared for anything."[114]

"Anything" turned out to be much less volcanic than anyone had expected. Hopper's reactions to the new cut ranged and raged and varied over the next hour and a half, from the exasperated "You've turned this into a television film," to the resigned "It's fine—it's good," to surprisingly, the ecstatic "That's beautiful! Don't ever, ever let me cut another film again."

Donn Cambern recalls that "Ultimately, there were just a couple places where Dennis felt the wrong person was talking or it should be on him, or whatever. He was very easy to accommodate."[115]

A final, and vital, element which made *Easy Rider, Easy Rider,* was the music. As noted in the previous chapter, the soundtrack of *Easy Rider* is a grab-bag collage of late-1960s psychedelia, R&B, folk, country, rock 'n' roll, and even some oddball and definitely of-its-time novelty material. Those songs are pretty damn close to what a 1960s version of Jack Kerouac might have heard on underground FM radio as he blew across America in 1968, which, perhaps inadvertently, was the whole point.

"Dennis and I agreed that we should cut the film with music behind the rides to fill in the track and lend emotion to the vision. We began by using music from our own record collection. It worked beyond anything we could imagine," Fonda has said.[116]

In spite of the immediate and organic way in which these currently popular songs fed into the visuals, in 1968, no one had ever scored a mainstream movie with "found music" this way. Occasionally, a current song would find its way into the background of an American movie, perhaps as sampled on a character's car radio, for example. But usually, all of the music behind the film was created by that film's composer for the sake of "harmonic unity," and perhaps because that composer, and the studio he worked for, were hoping to get a hit song out of that film, which they would then control. In *Rebel Without a Cause* (1955), for example, when James Dean switches on his car radio, it isn't rock 'n' roll he is listening to, as one would expect, but rather Leonard Rosenman's (that film's composer) icky symphonic backgrounds, which Dean's parents might have enjoyed very much.

True to form, Fonda and Hopper ultimately intended to create an original score for *Easy Rider* as well. Original rock 'n' roll scores had occasionally been used in the 1960s, and even before. *The Graduate* (1967), for example, utilized wall-to-wall Simon & Garfunkel songs, both preexisting and original.

For this purpose, Fonda, after apparently being turned down by The Band, decided that Crosby, Stills & Nash would be perfect. He described the movie to them, and they became very excited about working on the project. Fonda was already friends with David Crosby, too. In fact, Fonda once claimed that the marijuana used on-screen in the movie was courtesy of Crosby, and Crosby, for his part, has claimed that Hopper's physical appearance in the film—the handlebar mustache and the cowboy swagger that Hopper affected in the film—was modeled on *his* look. These factors, one would think, should certainly have given David Crosby's band the inside track.

There was one problem, though. Its name was Dennis Hopper.

Hopper saw the band arrive at the studio in a limousine, which apparently rubbed him the wrong way. He told Stephen Stills that "anybody who rides in a limo can't comprehend my movie, so I'm gonna have to say no to this, and if you guys try to get in the studio again, I may have to cause you some bodily harm."[117] As suspicious as this story sounds, even considering that we are talking about Dennis Hopper, Hopper himself repeated it several times over the years, and with some pride, so it might be somewhat true. Fonda has suggested, however, that the band itself bowed out when they realized they would never be able to improve upon the film's "found music" soundtrack, which was still in place when he showed them the movie. At some point during this period, someone suggested that, well, then, why couldn't they just keep that existing soundtrack?

Could they? As is sometimes the case when something has never been done before, the answer turned out to be "yes," because at the time, using a song in a movie was still considered the same as playing it on the radio. It was considered to be a good way to promote the song, and it was considered to be free.

"In those days, because nobody had ever used music, found music, all you had to do was go ask the artist for permission. You didn't have to pay the record company or anybody; it was amazing," Hopper said in 1995.[118] Peter Fonda, however, tells us that ultimately the artists *were* paid, a thousand dollars each. Still a bargain, considering what the film gained from the participation of those artists—all of whom had to be shown the movie. Fonda recalls that John Kay, of Steppenwolf, sat in the screening room wearing dark Wayfarer sunglasses throughout the entire film. "The end of the movie comes and John Kay turns around to me and says, 'Was that in color?' He's color-blind—that's the glasses. I said, 'Yeah.' He said, 'Show it to the Russians in black-and-white. It'll blow their mind!"[119]

Cambern, in particular, who had once been a music editor, had very practical ideas about how to rhythmically cut the imagery to those songs.

I had a good concept in mind of how to make the cuts rhythmic without repeating yourself, of not always cutting to a new scene on the downbeat of the bar. Sometimes I would cut into the downbeat on the fourth beat, the kicker beat, depending on the essence of the content; sometimes it would last for maybe two bars. I would still make the cut on the strong beat, which could be the downbeat, the third beat, or the kicker beat. And when you look at those sequences with that in mind, you'll see how it plays so beautifully. Look, and listen, to the scene of Peter on the motorcycle with Jack—wonderful![120]

After *Easy Rider*'s success, and significantly, the success of *Easy Rider*'s soundtrack, these musical loopholes were silenced very quickly. For example, by the time of *American Graffiti* (1973), just four years later, the studio—this time Universal—ended up paying $90,000 to license the forty-two songs featured on the soundtrack.

Columbia, at this point, still wanted to throw *Easy Rider* into drive-ins, and move on. Steve Blauner, who had recently partnered with Rafelson and Schneider (leading to Raybert being rechristened BBS, for Bert, Bob, and Steve), remembered an uncomfortable dinner with Columbia executive Jerry Heims.

He was sitting there like somebody had died, *and if he smiled his lips were going to crack and he was going to bleed. "What's Bert doing to his father?" he said.*

"What's Bert doing to his father?" I said. "He's probably going to keep him in business. Don't you understand what you have here? Look, the worst thing you have is a biker movie, which you paid half a million dollars for, up front, which will gross $6 to $10 million. But if it crosses over, which I think it might, who knows?"

He looked at me like I was insane.[121]

With *Easy Rider* essentially finished, the film could now be screened for Columbia executives. The studio brass all filed into the big screening room on the lot on a Friday afternoon. Cambern, who was there to control the volume levels on the print, which had not been locked yet, remembers that

> *The studio's vice president in charge of physical production, John Leech, who I'd see around the lot sometimes, would always glare at me. My hair was down to my shoulders, and he'd give me the evilest "you dirty hippie" look you've ever seen in your life.*
>
> *So we ran the movie. And we finished, and there was a long pause. Leo Jaffe, chairman of the board of Columbia Pictures, stood up and said, "I don't know what the fuck it's all about, but it's going to make a fuck of a lot of money." And on the way out, Leech, the VP that I thought hated me, came up, all smiles, and said, "Donn, I hear we have a wonderful, smash film."*
>
> *What an extraordinary picture-business moment, you know.*[122]

On top of this radical sea change in *Easy Rider*'s favor, Hopper, as he had long dreamed, somehow managed to get his film booked at Cannes. This one-two punch finally forced the studio to rethink its strategy of throwing the film away—although even at this point, there was still some reluctance to spend much money on a film produced by outsiders, and which many insiders, frankly, still did not "get." "But that was when Columbia executives stopped shaking their heads in incomprehension, and began nodding their heads in incomprehension," Fonda has said.[123]

While at Cannes, Hopper and Fonda submitted to a press conference, seated on motorcycles and trying—and failing—to converse with the natives in French. Fonda, now sporting a bushy beard, rented a Civil War cavalry general's uniform for the film's French premiere screening, which he stated had something to do with the state of civil unrest in the United States. The picture itself ultimately nabbed Hopper an award for Best Film by a New Director, which of course had been a lifelong dream.

Back in Hollywood, Columbia now prepared a print ad which contained the iconic text "A man went looking for America, and couldn't find it anywhere." Clearly someone working for publicity director John C. Flynn, presumably under age sixty, must have come up with this. The striking artwork underneath—which featured Fonda alone, no Dennis Hopper, and significantly, no motorcycles in sight—also highlighted the Cannes win. Clearly, the studio was trying to say that this picture was not another *Hells Angels on Wheels*.

The Columbia Pictures official publicity kit for the picture is remarkable for its earnest, confused, and almost apologetic tone:

> Easy Rider *is structured as both an odyssey and a ballad. It chronicles the cross-country journey of two young men who would currently be labeled "hippies." Their search for "freedom" results in a number of encounters with the people of America, each encounter (stanza) being joined to the next by a reprise of lyrical motorcycle riding.*
>
> *Because knowing more in advance about* Easy Rider *would deprive you of the initial experience of discovery, it is suggested that you defer reading this attached synopsis until you have seen the film itself.*

Later on, the same document mentions with awe that "Before it was finished the film would entail the travel of thousands of miles and the utilization of the largest motion picture set ever devised—the entire southwestern portion of the United States. Early in the proceedings, it was decided that there would be no studio shooting. All filming would take place in actual locations, the feeling being that to shoot a picture of this type in the confines of a Hollywood soundstage would be to completely stifle the creativity of the personalities involved."

The official production notes for the studio, under Flynn's byline, state that "the story is as difficult to describe as freedom is to define. Basically, that is what the story is—freedom. The complete freedom so yearned for by a large segment of the youthful population today. Probably the two key words in the story of *Easy Rider* are 'freedom' and 'today,'" Flynn's ghostwriter asserts.

Beyond this minimal effort, the studio was still clearly reluctant to spend much money on advertising the picture. Fonda complained about

This study of a rather pensive Wyatt (Peter Fonda) was later adapted into the subsequent, and legendary, "A man went looking . . ." artwork (below). (©COLUMBIA PICTURES; PHOTOGRAPHER: PETER SOREL. COLUMBIA PICTURES/PHOTOFEST)

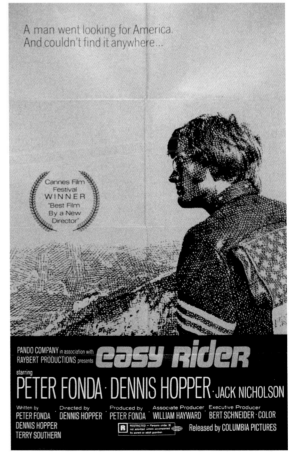

Variations on these images of Peter Fonda, Dennis Hopper, their iconic motorcycles, and the open road have adorned college dorm rooms, political cartoons, film satires, roadhouses, and many a biker's imagination for generations. (©COLUMBIA PICTURES; PHOTOGRAPHER: PETER SOREL. COLUMBIA PICTURES/PHOTOFEST)

Peter Fonda, who starred as Wyatt and produced and co-wrote *Easy Rider*, had appeared in motorcycle movies even before this one. These biker films successfully rescued his career from its earlier, clean-cut young man typecasting. (©COLUMBIA PICTURES; PHOTOGRAPHER: PETER SOREL. COLUMBIA PICTURES/PHOTOFEST)

As George Hanson, Jack Nicholson went into *Easy Rider* a failed actor and emerged from the experience a star. (©COLUMBIA PICTURES; COLUMBIA PICTURES/PHOTOFEST)

Dennis Hopper, who played Billy and also co-wrote and directed the film, represented the hedonistic side of the 1960s, capturing the spirit of both outlaw bikers and the vanished American frontier. (©COLUMBIA PICTURES; COLUMBIA PICTURES/PHOTOFEST)

Hopper, Luke Askew, and Fonda on the New Mexico commune set, portrayed by the Santa Monica Mountains above Los Angeles. Fonda later contracted pneumonia—according to studio publicity, from an allergic reaction to those innocent-looking bales of hay behind his head. (©COLUMBIA PICTURES; PHOTOGRAPHER: PETER SOREL. COLUMBIA PICTURES/PHOTOFEST)

Luke Askew, as the unnamed and enigmatic "Stranger on the Highway," lives up to his name. The building behind him is still there, but is no longer a gas station. (UPPER PHOTO: ©COLUMBIA PICTURES; PHOTOGRAPHER: PETER SOREL. COLUMBIA PICTURES/PHOTOFEST. LOWER PHOTO: COURTESY OF ALAN DUNN, 2009)

Music producer Phil Spector was a friend of the filmmakers who agreed to appear as a jittery drug buyer. Forty years later, Spector would be arrested for a different, and much more serious, crime. (©COLUMBIA PICTURES; COLUMBIA PICTURES/PHOTOFEST)

Cinematographer László Kovács, seen here with his director, forever changed the look and texture of American films. (©COLUMBIA PICTURES; COLUMBIA PICTURES/PHOTOFEST)

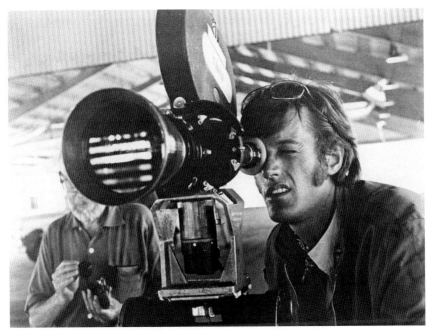

Producer Fonda lines up a shot, perhaps because director Hopper is nowhere to be seen. (©COLUMBIA PICTURES; COLUMBIA PICTURES/PHOTOFEST)

A Hollywood movie on location, even a low-budget one, always attracts crowds of curious locals, none of whom Peter Fonda and Dennis Hopper appear to notice here. Note, however, that Hopper seems to be seated not on his own cycle, but on Fonda's Captain America bike. (©COLUMBIA PICTURES; COLUMBIA PICTURES/PHOTOFEST)

Easy Rider is a road film which includes many off-road campfire scenes. Top: Fonda, Nicholson, and Hopper seem amused by something which is happening off camera. Bottom: Hopper, on second thought, is perhaps not so amused. (©COLUMBIA PICTURES; COLUMBIA PICTURES/ PHOTOFEST)

Hopper, Nicholson, and Fonda in the cage. Note the name "H. D. Stanton" behind Dennis's head, a shout-out to fellow actor Harry Dean Stanton. (©COLUMBIA PICTURES; PHOTOGRAPHER: PETER SOREL. COLUMBIA PICTURES/PHOTOFEST)

The prison interiors were shot in Taos, New Mexico; the exterior scenes, however, were filmed in Las Vegas, New Mexico. The former police station (right) is now an exclusive art gallery. (COURTESY OF JIM GRIFFIN, 2011)

Still on the road, easy riders Dennis Hopper, Peter Fonda, and Jack Nicholson. (©COLUMBIA PICTURES; PHOTOGRAPHER: PETER SOREL. COLUMBIA PICTURES/PHOTOFEST)

The tension between the filmmakers and the locals in Morganza, Louisiana, is apparent here. Dennis Hopper, however, still finds a moment to relax with a refreshing can of Jax beer.

Like their on-screen characters, Hopper, Nicholson, and Fonda found the reception chilly inside Melancon's Café. (©COLUMBIA PICTURES; PHOTOGRAPHER: PETER SOREL. COLUMBIA PICTURES/PHOTOFEST)

Behind the scenes, outside Melancon's Café: The local teenagers' insistence on flocking around the motorcycles did very little to endear the filmmakers to their wary parents. (©COLUMBIA PICTURES; COLUMBIA PICTURES/PHOTOFEST)

Former site of Melancon's Cafe
1968 filming of the movie *Easy Rider*
Featuring: Peter Fonda, Dennis Hopper and
Jack Nicholson
Local Stars: Buddy Causey, Jr., Blaze Dawson,
Cynthia Grezaffi, P.J. Guedry, Jr., Elida Ann Hebert,
Mary Kaye Hebert, Arnold Hess, Jr., Duffy Lafont,
Rose LeBlanc, Colette Purpera, Susie Ramagos,
Hayward Robillard

The citizens of Morganza, who in 1968 had been less than completely hospitable to the *Easy Rider* crew, in 2010 put up a monument to the memory of that production on the vacant lot where Melancon's Café had stood. (COURTESY OF JIM GRIFFIN)

In April 2019, to commemorate the fiftieth anniversary of *Easy Rider*, a painted reconstruction of Melancon's Café was placed above the café's original steps. (COURTESY OF NATALIE THOMPSON)

Easy Rider's climactic scenes—and Wyatt and Billy—were shot on the outskirts of Krotz Springs, Louisiana. (©COLUMBIA PICTURES; PHOTOGRAPHER: PETER SOREL. COLUMBIA PICTURES/PHOTOFEST)

Alan Dunn, and a Captain America motorcycle, visit the Krotz Springs murder site in 2013. (COURTESY OF ALAN DUNN)

The Cannes Film Festival in May of 1969 was an early triumph for *Easy Rider*. Here Hopper, Fonda, and Nicholson celebrate their movie's win as "Best Film by a New Director," with fellow attendees Feliciano and J. Jefferson. (PHOTOFEST)

Dennis Hopper's gravesite, Taos, New Mexico, 2015. (COURTESY OF ALAN DUNN)

how the company refused to spend a dime, initially, on either television or radio spots, while lavishing millions on Columbia's big releases of the year, *McKenna's Gold* and *Marooned*, both of which starred the fifty-three-year-old Gregory Peck, a contemporary of Fonda's father.

To the studio's credit, Columbia had successfully released Paul Mazursky's wife-swapping comedy *Bob and Carol and Ted and Alice* earlier in the year. While that film starred thirty-one-year-old Natalie Wood (about the same age as Fonda and Hopper), by 1969, she had seemingly been a star almost as long as Gregory Peck, so therefore would have seemed "safe" to middle-class, and middle-aged, audiences.

Easy Rider was something else entirely. Although Columbia Pictures may not have understood—or even particularly supported—the picture, the very fact that it *was* a Columbia film, that it was being released by one of Hollywood's mighty majors, gave it far more cachet than an American International release could have, or even than the Cannes attention had.

That studio's considerable distribution and advertising muscle, even blunted by ambivalence, didn't hurt either. As Fonda has noted, Terry Southern's name in the screenwriting credits probably gave the film a limited, but important, measure of prestige as well, at least among the intelligentsia, to whom Southern's name would have signified that this truly was not just a motorcycle flick.

In 1969 the term *independent film* (just like *Cannes* and *Terry Southern*) wouldn't have meant anything to mainstream audiences. And these audiences, outside of a limited number of people in a few urban or college areas, probably never would have had the opportunity to see such a creature anyway. Most American film theaters at the time played only "American"—meaning, only Hollywood—films.

So, for these audiences, the point of reference for what a movie was would have been shaped *entirely* by the output of Columbia Pictures, and six other companies, and to a much lesser degree by upstarts like AIP, all of which were physically located in the same geographic region, and all of which shared the same small and clannish community of directors, technicians, actors, studio executives, composers, screenwriters, and theaters. Moreover, Hollywood, and Hollywood product, offered a more or less consistent point of view about ethics and morality and history and political science, and about what used to be ominously called "social engineering," as well.

In 1969, the stories Hollywood chose to tell, and the way they told them, had hardly changed for fifty years.

It was about to.

CHAPTER FOUR

Explosions and Implosions

WHILE COLUMBIA EXECUTIVES FUSSED OVER OR TRIED TO IGNORE *EASY Rider*, "within the counterculture, word began to build," writer Peter Biskind remarked. Columbia Pictures, in spite of its failings, did think to cannily fan these underground flames by offering prerelease screenings in college towns and in places where those in tune with the film's message could see it and spread the word.

Biskind relates how on the set of *They Shoot Horses, Don't They?* (1969), Jane Fonda had a conversation with Bruce Dern, whose photo of himself and Peter had inspired *Easy Rider's* conception.

> *"Wait'll you see Peter's movie," [Jane said]. "You're gonna freak out, 'cause there's a guy in that movie who is so fantastic; somebody has finally made a good biker movie."*
>
> *"Whaddya mean, a biker movie," [Bruce said]. "We made all the biker movies. I did eleven of them; it's over for biker movies."*
>
> *"No, this one's different."*
>
> *"Who's in it?"*
>
> *"Dennis, and this guy, Jack Nicholson."*
>
> *"Jack Nicholson? I gotta pay attention to this guy, Jack fuckin' Nicholson; he's gonna be a movie star?"*
>
> *Sure enough, six months later, he was.*[124]

Easy Rider opened on July 14, 1969, at the Beekman Theatre in Manhattan. Steve Blauner marveled that "From the opening day there were lines around the block. People who had never been to the East Side in their lives, people with no shoes, with sandals. They had to take the doors off the stalls in the men's room because they were in there smoking dope, whatever. And of course, the rest was history."[125]

Fonda also watched the throngs of hippies clawing their way through the doors. "We made all of our money back the first week. In one theater," he has often remarked.

Karen Black remembered, in 2003, that "when you went to see a movie like *Easy Rider*, and when you saw these guys really smoking grass by the fire, and the camaraderie was real and warm, you went: What the hell am I looking at? This has value. This has a completely different kind of value than *Pillow Talk*. This is something extraordinary. I want more of that."[126]

Most of the legitimate reviews were positive, as well—possibly, it must be said, because many mainstream critics were now afraid to appear un-hip or out of touch to their readers, especially their younger readers. This had been made abundantly clear in 1967, when Bosley Crowther, the undisputed dean of American film writers, had panned *Bonnie and Clyde*, that year's *cause célèbre* among young audiences, as "a pointless . . . bleeding farce of brutal killings."[127] Crowther's failure to "get it" made him look like a hopelessly out-of-date establishment fuddy-duddy. The result was that the sixty-four-year-old journalist was unceremoniously fired from his job at the *New York Times*, a job he had held since 1940, which, suddenly, no longer seemed like a good thing.

As to *Easy Rider*, the *New York Times* itself, with Vincent Canby (then in his mid-forties) at Crowther's old desk, remarked, apparently with an eye on job security, that "the rock score, the lovely, sometimes impressionistic photography by László Kovács, the faces of small-town America. These things not only are continually compelling but occasionally they dazzle the senses,"[128] although, to his credit, Canby's review, overall, was decidedly mixed.

Ellen Willis in *The New York Review of Books* wrote that "*Easy Rider* is about the failure of America on all levels, hip and straight. Billy and Wyatt on their bikes, riding free down the open road, are living another version of the rugged individualist frontier fantasy, and the big dope deal that made them financially independent is just hip capitalism. It won't work."[129] Ms. Willis's unusually insightful review was written when she was twenty-eight.

Across town in *The Village Voice*, an uncredited critic damned the movie with faint praise, and a lot of verbiage, by remarking that "with all the rousingly rhythmic revelry and splendiferously scenic motorcycling, *Easy Rider* comes to resemble a perpetual pre-credit sequence, but reasonably pleasant withal."[130]

The much more middlebrow *Life*, which was still the nation's magazine in 1969 (but not for much longer), was generally positive in their review. Critic Richard Schickel wrote that "the film has a marvelous quality of being alive to its own possibilities, good and bad, of the land it moves against."[131] Which meant, presumably, that Schickel liked it?

Pauline Kael, the very influential *New Yorker* critic, was also intellectually ambivalent about *Easy Rider*. "What is new about *Easy Rider* is not necessarily that one finds its attitudes appealing but that the movie conveys the mood of the drug culture with such skill and in such full belief that these simplicities are the truth that one can understand why these attitudes are appealing to others. *Easy Rider* is an expression and a confirmation of how this audience feels; the movie attracts a new kind of 'inside' audience, whose members enjoy tuning in together to a whole complex of shared signals and attitudes."[132]

The New Republic's Stanley Kaufman also wrote a largely positive review of the film, but quibbled over the "We blew it" scene. "Why by any values that they show in the film," he carps, "had they blown it?"[133]

Reflecting the largely stoned clientele now finding its way to the Beekman, and now other theaters across the nation as well, *Esquire's* Jacob Brackman amusingly remarked that "it's inconsequential, I suppose, whether anyone herein connected was actually blowing anything illegal, except if they weren't, they all deserve Oscars. If they were, well, what the hell."[134]

Film Comment's Charles C. Hampton remarked that the strength of the movie is how the "straight world and the head world collide." He then proceeded to answer—at least to his own satisfaction, if to no one else's—a question which audiences are still asking. "'We blew it,'" he said, "refers to the characters' inability to exist in both worlds."[135]

In *Sight and Sound*, Tom Milne perhaps too colorfully remarked that the film "succeeds where it matters most, in communicating a yearning vision of a different way of life, in an America seen as a vast, unexplored representation of beauty, optimism and adventure."[136]

In *Artforum*, another influential critic, Manny Farber, remarked that "Dennis Hopper's lyrical, quirky film is better than pretty good in its handling of death, both the actual event and in the way the lead acting, like Ryan–Holden's [meaning Robert Ryan and William Holden] in *The Wild Bunch*, and Shirley Knight's in *The Rain People*, carries a scent of death."[137] While interesting, Faber's very scent-concerned comments didn't really reveal whether the critic actually liked the movie or not.

Joel Haycock at the *Harvard Crimson* said that "technically, *Easy Rider* is a clumsy first picture. Hopper breaks directorial line in almost every sequence to no valuable effect. Kovács's landscapes and wide-angle shots of the two motorcycles crossing the Southwest are quite marvelous; but the LSD sequence is predictable—lots of fish-eye shots, weeping, and intimation of death—and boring, and doesn't do justice to the drug."[138] (Obviously a college paper.) Haycock also, apparently alone among critics, criticized Hopper and Cambern's innovative editing flourishes by commenting on how "Hopper also has an irritating editing affectation: when indicating the passage of time, he'll cut two [*sic*] frames of the next sequence in twice at the end of the preceding scene. Real avant-garde."[139]

On the other hand, Roger Ebert, already the critic for the *Chicago Sun-Times* but not yet the all-media superstar he would become, was unstinting in his praise. "Someday it was inevitable that a great film would come along, utilizing the motorcycle genre, the same way the great Westerns suddenly made everyone realize they were a legitimate American art form; *Easy Rider* is the picture."[140] Ebert, it should be noted, was twenty-seven at the time.

Closer to home, in the *Los Angeles Times*, Charles Champlin could have been on the payroll of the Columbia Pictures publicity department when he raved that "from its deceptively amusing beginnings to its swift and terrible end, *Easy Rider* is an astonishing work of art and an overpowering motion picture experience. It is also a social document which is poignant, potent, disturbing and important."[141]

Variety, the venerable Hollywood trade paper, offered more of a summation of the film than a review, as was the paper's habit, so that players at Hollywood parties who hadn't seen the film could pretend they had. Critic Gene Moskowitz, who signed his reviews "Mosk," did comment that "Fonda exudes a groping moral force and Hopper is agitated, touching and responsive as the sidekick."[142]

Across town at *The Hollywood Reporter*, John Mahoney said that "*Easy Rider* is very likely the cleanest and most disturbing picture of the angry estrangement of American youth to be brought to the screen."[143] Apparently, Mahoney thought he was still reviewing *Rebel Without a Cause*.

At the *Hollywood Citizen News* Todd Everett said the film has "all the sheen of a well-made B-picture."[144] Although, interestingly, he also mentioned that "Peter Fonda has come to bear much the same relationship with the motorcycle picture that John Wayne has to the Western, the rugged, handsome, prototypical hero."[145]

At the *Motion Picture Herald* Richard Gertner told his readers that "the film strives for poetry (and many times achieves it). And it makes an explicit statement on some of the sicknesses which are eating away at the heart of our country today."[146] Gertner did call out Hopper's acid trip sequence as "simply too long and overdone," however.[147]

Both *Film Quarterly* and the *Los Angeles Herald Examiner* liked *Easy Rider*, but in an "only in California" aside, both criticized the film for its "ridiculous presentation of mime,"[148] which, as the *Herald Tribune*'s Winfred Blevins melodramatically implored, "millions would be offended by."[149] Likewise, *Film Quarterly*'s Harriet R. Polk snorted through her nose that "the mime troupe which suddenly appears is not only implausible, but faintly embarrassing. A bit of Los Angeles 'culture' worked up for the commune sequence, which seems to have been shot somewhere in the LA hills."[150]

Surprisingly, and as can be noted from the samples above, few reviews of *Easy Rider* were completely negative. Bucking the trend, the *Miami Herald*'s James E. Meyer carped that "Ten minutes after *Easy Rider* began, I started watch-watching. It was then that I knew I was going to be in for a bad time. Fortunately, I had only eighty-five minutes to go." He concluded by admitting that "the under-25 group may dig this the most. As one of the over-30 boys, I must report it left me fuming, fussing and fidgeting."[151]

In *Focus*, Charles Flynn lamented that "every other line of dialogue begins with 'man,' every sequence ends with the same shot of Fonda and Hopper on the motorcycles."[152] Flynn goes on to say that "actually, *Easy Rider* is more about Fonda/Hopper's devotion to their bikes than anything else. They see the machines as phallic extensions of themselves." Flynn finally put his poison pen down after remarking that "this is an incredibly heavy-handed, simple-minded, amateurish, awkward, [Stanley] Kramer-ish film."[153]

Show magazine utilized a very unusual tactic in discussing the film; they asked a college student (USC Class of '73), one O'Connel Driscoll, who presumably was exactly the film's target demographic, about *Easy Rider*. Unlike most older critics above, who largely were afraid of accusations of not being "with it," Driscoll called it as he saw it, found sham and phoniness on the open road, and wondered if what his fellow students bought into was the advertising campaign. "Maybe there wasn't any movie here," he began, before asking his readers to "picture Peter Fonda and Dennis Hopper, gliding along, side by side, sort of like Rock Hudson and Sandra Dee on water skis. That's what you've got when you mount your basic Culver City–type cinematographer on back of your basic Culver City reflector-equipped camera truck."[154]

An older and more subtle critic turned out to be the vice president of the United States, Spiro Agnew, who didn't mention *Easy Rider* by name, but must have been referring to Captain America and Billy when he mentioned at a rally in September 1970, in Las Vegas, Nevada, a current film promoting as heroes "two men who are able to live a carefree life off the proceeds of illegal sales of drugs."[155] He went on to condemn Hollywood in general because, as he put it, "far too many producers and editors are still succumbing to the temptation of the sensational and playing right into the hands of the drug culture."[156] Agnew then concluded his unorthodox "review" by urging the election of "square" Republicans" as a reliable solution to that problem.

Some unkind reviews of the movie were more personal in their barbs. *Film Quarterly*, in a second review that same year, said that "where the film goes soft is in the creation of Peter Fonda's Wyatt, and this may be largely a result of Fonda's own influence on the making of the film . . . he seems to demand that every part he plays be a variation on Jesus Christ."[157]

Another even more personal critic of Peter Fonda was his own father. At Cannes, Peter was grilled about what Henry thought of the movie. "He really loves it," Peter said, in very broken (actually, nonexistent) French. Bill Hayward also claimed that Peter's dad appreciated the film, although perhaps that the older Fonda was reluctant to admit this to his son. But the elder Fonda's opinions were actually much more complex than that. Peter told *The Daily Camera* in 2013 that "I had him come down and look at an early cut. We had to get Dennis out of the room to get it below four hours. My dad watched it and then I went over the next day to his house. He was very serious. He said, 'Look, son, I know you have all your eggs in this basket. And I'm worried about it because the film is inaccessible. We don't see where you're going, and why. . . . I just don't think many people will get it.'"[158]

Incidentally, the older Fonda did not "get" Dennis Hopper, either. In 1970 he told the *New York Times* that "the man is an idiot. I will not work with Dennis, because I won't put up with his s—t. He's a total freak-out, stoned out of his mind all the time. Any man who insists on wearing his cowboy hat to the Academy Award ceremonies and keeps it on at the dinner table afterward ought to be spanked."[159]

When Hopper heard this, he exclaimed, "Henry Fonda said I was an idiot? I guess it just goes to show you what the establishment view of me is. Of course, I did make his son a star in *Easy Rider*. But so far as Henry Fonda's not wanting to work with me, he doesn't really have to worry. Because, frankly, I find the man a bore. He hasn't done a good movie in ten years. I admired him in *The Grapes of Wrath*, but I'd say he had a pretty good director there in John Ford, wouldn't you?"[160]

At the box office, which trumps the reviews and the infighting every time, *Easy Rider* ultimately earned $19.1 million in theatrical rentals in the United States alone. Fonda believes that it was considerably more than that, but this is the number Columbia Pictures has always admitted to. The cumulative worldwide gross (box office ticket sales) has been estimated at $60 million, approximately $41 million of which was earned domestically. That number, for reference, is the equivalent of more than $400 million in today's ticket prices.

In 1969, *Easy Rider* was Columbia's most successful film of the year, and the fourth-highest-grossing picture of 1969, overall. Ultimately *Easy Rider* would become the twenty-eighth-highest-grossing film of the decade. And remember that all of this windfall was from a film whose entire budget was considerably less than $500,000.

With all of this easy money pouring into the coffers at Columbia, it became apparent to the delighted studio that it could not be *just* young people going to see the film. Liberal-minded, college-educated adults must have been coming to see it too. People who disagreed with the film's viewpoint were now apparently buying tickets in order to disagree with the film's viewpoint. Teenagers and young adults were dragging their parents into the theater as well, along with under-seventeens lying at the box office to nearsighted ticket sellers in order to see what the R-rated fuss was all about.

This crossover appeal is very much comparable to what had happened a generation before with *Rebel Without a Cause*, which the parents of the *Easy Rider* generation had forced *their* parents to see in order to show them how *they* felt. Now these parents, with children of their own, were being asked by those children to see *Easy Rider*, and to try to remember.

The picture also did well, somewhat surprisingly, worldwide. "I thought *Easy Rider* could be a hit in America," Fonda said in 1970, "but it's done very well in Europe, which surprised me. It's shown there with subtitles, but the Europeans pick up everything that's going down. It played capacity business in places like Stockholm and Helsinki, for between six months and a year."[161] Years later, Fonda recalled with amazement that the film had played in one theater in Paris for almost five years. Hopper, in an act of apparent one-upmanship, claimed that the number of years the film ran in that same theater was actually twenty-five!

Eventually the film was dubbed into other languages as well. The always-difficult process of having to time equivalent French phrases, for example, into the mouths of actors originally speaking English was aggravated in this case by the fact that there were few instances of a separate effects tracks available, as original sound editor James Nelson didn't have the budget to create one, meaning that the original dialogue was recorded on the same track as the backgrounds. So, crickets and motorcycle motors and crackling campfires all had to be separately and expensively re-created so that a Gallic Dennis Hopper could say *homme* instead of "man."

Executives at Columbia Pictures, delighted at the continued box-office success of "their" picture, late in the year started noticing that counterculture audiences, or someone, was apparently creating their own artwork to advertise the film. Handmade, or hand-printed, notices started showing up on campuses and communes around the country. These looked like ad slicks for local clubs, but they were advertising a movie. Not an independent movie that needed grassroots support, but a film that already had its own well-funded marketing department behind it! Today, these crudely laid-out handbills are, as could be expected, valuable treasures for *Easy Rider* collectors, and sometimes are hard to separate from other fan art created decades later to celebrate those fans' self-perpetuating interest in all things *Easy Rider*.

Colorful posters and artwork, usually depicting those bikes in black-and-white, with Haight-Ashbury–style washes and psychedelic flourishes added, also started appearing in communes and dorm rooms and silk-screened onto T-shirts throughout this era, to the intense frustration of Columbia marketing executives, who could not figure out a way to collect residuals on any of these unauthorized and homegrown symbols of appreciation.

In the months after its release, *Easy Rider* was also co-opted by political cartoons and illustrators who depicted, for example, Richard Nixon and Spiro Agnew astride the Captain America and Billy bikes, often accompanied by the line "We blew it." *MAD* magazine, in June of 1970, did a parody called "Sleazy Riders," illustrated by Mort Drucker. Amusingly, in this satire, presumably aimed at the film's target demographic, the freaks were mocked as mercilessly as the straights were. More recently, *Peanuts'* Snoopy and Charlie Brown and *Looney Tunes'* Bugs Bunny and Yosemite Sam have been depicted as Captain America and Billy in printed or even animated cartoons as well.

As if shamed into it, late in the year Columbia's marketing department cheaply tweaked their own, by this point, already-iconic "A man went looking for America . . ." artwork to include the phrase "This year, it's Easy Rider."

This was true. In 1969, it was *Easy Rider*.

In 1969, it might be worthwhile to note, a man walked on the moon, Charles Manson's crazed cult murdered at least seven people, the Woodstock music festival was held in upstate New York, Richard Nixon was sworn in as president of the United States, the first Walmart opened, the first episode of *The Brady Bunch* and the last episode of the original *Star Trek* aired on American television, and the Beatles made their last public appearance, as did, after a fashion, Judy Garland, Dwight D. Eisenhower, Boris Karloff, Joseph P. Kennedy, and Jack Kerouac, all of whom passed away that year.

In the movies, there were also several trends peaking or waning in 1969, of which *Easy Rider* played a significant part.

Several Westerns, for example, were successful that year, perhaps the last year in that genre's long history in which that could truthfully be said. *True Grit*, *The Wild Bunch*, and *Butch Cassidy and the Sundance Kid*, for example, were all fabulously successful—although *Easy Rider's* connection to that genre, except among its creators, was only noticed after the fact.

Easy Rider is also an unheralded member of a type of film known as the "buddy movie," of which two of the most famous, *Midnight Cowboy* and *Butch Cassidy and the Sundance Kid*, came out the same year it did. Although again, it was not Wyatt and Billy's friendship, but rather the friendships depicted in those other two films, particularly *Butch Cassidy*, that would later be remarked upon as the instigator of a calculable trend.

But it could be said that in all other ways, *Easy Rider* did significantly and visibly affect its year, particularly in regard to other trends in filmmaking, popular culture, and music.

A soundtrack album featuring the songs of the movie was, of course, released when the movie became such a commercial success. Most of the artists on the soundtrack agreed to license their songs for the record (which, of course, was literally that—a black vinyl disc; remember those?).

Some of the artists, like Steppenwolf, were already on the Dunhill/ABC label, which was producing the soundtrack, but ultimately, five separate record companies had to be negotiated with in order to license all of the songs. A sixth label, Capitol Records, which managed The Band, ultimately could not be brought to terms, and so a sound-alike cover of "The Weight" by the band Smith, had to be substituted.

The *Easy Rider* album repeated the success of the *Easy Rider* movie. It came out in August 1969, and was certified gold in January 1970. Its medley of counterculture harmonies could be heard on the street outside communes and college dorm rooms and roadhouses and suburban tract houses throughout the 1970s.

Easy Rider was eventually nominated for Academy Awards for Best Original Screenplay and for Best Supporting Actor (Nicholson), both of which it lost.

The April 7, 1970, Oscars presentation came ten months after the opening, but the film was still playing widely in theaters in the United States and abroad. But by then, its continued—and to some, inexplicable—success inevitably tarnished *Easy Rider*'s reputation as a renegade underdog, which of course something so monstrously successful could not long remain.

About the same time, and for about the same reasons, the very counterculture which had first embraced *Easy Rider* as speaking in its own voice suddenly decided that the film had co-opted that voice to commercial ends. Regarding *Easy Rider*'s relationship to that segment of its audience, for example, author and screenwriter Buck Henry pointed out that "nobody knew who wrote it, nobody knew who directed it, nobody knew who edited it. Rip [Torn] was supposed to be in it. Jack [Nicholson] was in it instead. It looks like a couple hundred outtakes from several other films all strung together, with a soundtrack of the best of the '60s. But it opened up a path. Now the children of Dylan were in control."[162]

The truth is, of course, that *Easy Rider* wasn't trying to speak to, or for, a generation at all. *Easy Rider* wasn't willed into existence by the counterculture. The film reflected the opinions and experiences of an individual, like all art does (and in this case, it was at least *two* individuals). It isn't fair to accuse an artist of selling out a cause for commercial gain, and at the same time point out how that artist wasn't a part of that cause to begin with.

One thing that Buck Henry did get right is that, in the wake of *Easy Rider*, youth became an asset, especially in Hollywood. Suddenly, young people who had previously been working as office boys at Columbia Pictures found their opinions being actively solicited by their employers. These employers might not have liked or understood these bearded enigmas whom they were now certain coveted their carpeted offices from the other side of the generation gap, but they were certain that these kids somehow knew *something* they did not—although they had no idea what that something might be.

Most movies about the 1960s before this had been made by people who didn't understand, by filmmakers who were working in the decade, but were not *of* the decade. Many of these films were created by young, or youngish, filmmakers, like Paul Mazursky or Mike Nichols, or Richard Lester or Roger Corman, men who were looking, sympathetically or not, from the outside in, or, on the other side of the divide, or by old men like Otto Preminger or Michelangelo Antonioni or Hy Averback, who were actually mocking the mores of the counterculture, even while pretending to be part of it.

On the other side of the protest line were those movies made by filmmakers who understood what was going on around them all too well, but were such card-carrying outsiders that their viewpoint only turned out to be relevant during the era, or in movies about the era, or to people from the era. Talented, underappreciated filmmakers like Richard Rush, Tom Laughlin, or Michael Wadleigh come to mind, filmmakers who regretfully never fit in, or, one hopes, never hoped to fit in behind the studio gates.

Inside those studio gates, at least some executives took on some of the external trappings of the youth movement, and even employed some actual young people. Future executive Peter Guber, twenty-eight in 1970, suddenly noticed that his middle-aged bosses had started wearing love beads and sandals to the office, and were now soliciting his opinions. "My inexperience, lack of contacts, and relationships were not handicapping. Because of my youth people asked, 'Well, what do you think?'"[163] he recalls.

Director Paul Schrader remembered in 1999 that "*Easy Rider* was counterculture paranoia elevated to a kind of superficial Hollywood glossiness. The kids in bell-bottoms and beads making movies. And the whole Hollywood establishment had to stop and recess because at the exact same time that film had come up, Hollywood had just sunk millions into several very big clinkers, *Paint Your Wagon* (1969), *Hello, Dolly!* (1969). And here comes this film making a fortune; it changed the industry."[164]

The old guard which was giving way to the new went all the way to the top. Abraham Schneider, who resigned as chairman of the board at Columbia in 1973, stated that if *Easy Rider* was the way the industry was going to go, he did not understand it and did not want to be part of it. He would not be the last.

The people most affected by *Easy Rider*'s success, of course were its creators. Jack Nicholson, at the very moment of crisis when he was considering giving up acting altogether, instead became a movie star. And Peter Fonda and Dennis Hopper went from being total (if well-connected) outsiders to finding themselves dropped down the rabbit hole and into the weird but admirable position of suddenly *becoming* the moguls they had once battled against to get their movie made. The movies *they* then made, and the movies their contemporaries made, ideally capture the perils and pratfalls of taking on the system . . . and then winning.

Dennis Hopper's next project was something called *The Last Movie* (1971). Hopper was probably inspired by John Wayne's penchant from that era for making his Westerns in Durango, Mexico, one of the first of which was *The Sons of Katie Elder* (1965), which Hopper costarred in. While on location in Durango, Hopper noticed that the indigenous peoples, their local economy, and eventually, their identity and folklore, would all come to rely on these films, and on Hollywood—specifically, on John Wayne.

Thus inspired, Hopper's story involved a Hollywood stuntman (to be played by himself) on location for a Western shooting in Peru who stays behind after the film crew returns home.

For the star and director in his film-within-a-film, Hopper wanted to cast Wayne and Henry Hathaway, who had directed them both in *Katie*

Elder and *True Grit*. Dennis Hopper and John Wayne had an interesting relationship, which was not as adversarial as one might think. Wayne did like to refer to Hopper as "that pinko," and surprisingly, the nickname was not without some degree of begrudging affection. Hopper, for his part, once mused about Wayne: "Is it possible not to like the man? You know, he's like the character I play in *The Last Movie*. Naive, innocent, blindly American, a guy with preconceived notions about everything. Paranoid and afraid of everything that's different."[165]

Wayne and Hathaway, regretfully, and not at all unexpectedly, both passed on *The Last Movie*, but Hopper did talk a lot of friends into getting involved, along with a lot of strangers who were attracted to the prospect of working with Hollywood's new messiah. They all made the trek to South America to realize Hopper's fevered vision, although most were little used or nearly unrecognizable in the film. *The Last Movie* RSVP list finally grew to include Julie Adams, Sylvia Miles, director Sam Fuller, Henry Jaglom, Michelle Phillips (who, over eight surely memorable days, Hopper would marry and divorce in 1970—"The first seven were pretty good," he would joke), Kris Kristofferson, Dean Stockwell, Russ Tamblyn, James Mitchum (Robert Mitchum's offspring), John Phillip Law, and even Peter Fonda.

Filmed 4,100 miles from Hollywood, with a lavish budget and no one to say no to his excesses, Hopper was able to indulge in the flourishes and fantasies which had largely been denied him from Monument Valley to Mardi Gras. "Stylistically, *The Last Movie* is," as Winkler observed, "like the cemetery sequence in *Easy Rider* writ large. Taking Godard to heart, Hopper imposed a nonlinear structure on *The Last Movie*, which has a beginning, a middle, and an end, but not in that order."[166]

Not even "the new Hollywood" was ready for this. Universal, the studio which had been unlucky enough to finance *The Last Movie*, not surprisingly, hated it, didn't get it, and didn't want it. Audiences—even college audiences, who should have at least pretended to be receptive to the film—were as confused as their parents would have been. *The Last Movie* was a critical and financial disaster, although it is entirely possible there is a good movie in there somewhere. It single-handedly nailed closed all the doors which *Easy Rider* had blown open for Dennis Hopper.

Peter Fonda's next project, which this time, not surprisingly, he directed himself, was *The Hired Hand* (1971). Although sometimes dismissed in reviews of the time as an acid or "hippie Western," the simple story about two cowboys (Fonda and buddy/frequent costar Warren Oates) trying to mend fences and marriages, could not have been more traditional, although the elegiac photography (by Vilmos Zsigmond) and poetic, layered screenplay (by Alan Sharp) were unusual, and unusually subtle, for such a seemingly traditional genre offering.

Fonda shot some of the film on location in New Mexico. Unfortunately, *Easy Rider* was playing at a drive-in a little too near the location, so the ghost of that film, and the sound of hundreds of car speakers blasting "Don't Bogart That Joint" across the desert, kept interfering with the tender scene the director was trying to capture.

Back in Hollywood, for the movie's release, Universal Studios took out a huge billboard near the Chateau Marmont on the Sunset Strip to publicize the film. Peter Fonda was horrified when he saw it. "It had a cutout of my naked torso coming up over the top with a cowboy hat on and my legs tied up in rope, guns stuck in my belt, and it said THAT EASY RIDER IS RIDING AGAIN, RIDING FAST AND HARD ACROSS THE WEST."[167] Horrified, Fonda forced studio big boss Lew Wasserman to take the expensive sign down.

Unfortunately, *The Hired Hand* was almost as big a flop for Universal as *The Last Movie* had been. It is, however, a fine and much more accessible film.

At least Fonda and Hopper tried to do something different. All around them, at all seven of the studios, youth films, which had once been left to Roger Corman and AIP, were suddenly in vogue. *Rebel Without a Cause* had been in some ways the first film about a teenager who was not aspiring to be just like his parents. But the AIP cycle of "beach movies," the "Tammy" films (of which Peter Fonda had been a survivor), the "Gidget" films, and more-adult fare like *A Summer Place* (1959) had largely backslid. Frankie Avalon, after all, was, more or less, Andy Hardy in a swimsuit.

In the early 1970s, however, partially thanks to the considerably older Wyatt and Billy, teenagers were allowed to grow up and have problems.

Last Summer (1969), *Bless the Beasts and Children* (1971), *Friends* (1971), *Murmur of the Heart* (1971), *Summer of '42* (1971), and, of course, *American Graffiti* (1973), all allowed teenagers to love and fight and even kill each other.

And these movies were cheap to make—which caused Hollywood to almost tear itself apart trying to make them, or find people who understood them to make them. The big-budget road-show movies which had followed in the wake of *The Sound of Music* (1965) suddenly, instead of merely being colossally unsuccessful, were now hopelessly passé as well. Wags at the time called *Easy Rider* "the little movie that killed the big picture." It was.

This new youth genre, if it could be called that, immediately splintered into several subspecies. There were the counterculture films, which featured communes and hippies and love beads and love-ins. Several of these came out before *Easy Rider*, but these predecessor films were all made by people who were unsympathetic, or who fundamentally misunderstood the cause they were mocking or celebrating. *I Love You, Alice B. Toklas!*, *Skidoo*, and *Maryjane* (all 1968) are a few of the more knuckleheaded examples. Many more of this type of film came out after *Easy Rider*. *The Strawberry Statement* and *The Magic Garden of Stanley Sweetheart* (both 1970), *Dusty and Sweets McGee*, *Taking Off*, *The Star-Spangled Girl*, and *Zabriskie Point* (all 1971) stand out somewhat, if not because of their content, then because of their psychedelic titles. *Billy Jack* (again, 1971) was an obvious *Easy Rider* variation, even though an earlier film, *Born Losers* (1967), had actually introduced the karate-kicking, paradoxically peace-loving Billy Jack character.

Then there are the biker films. This genre predated *Easy Rider* as well, and despite what Bruce Dern assumed, continued after it, without significant modification to the formula. Dennis Hopper once confided to Roger Ebert that an executive at 20th Century Fox had told him in the early 1970s that "every producer in town has his nephew out in the desert shooting a motorcycle picture."[168]

Most of these motorcycle pictures were outlaw biker gang tales, and so the counterculture itself was mostly set dressing, although a few of these films dealt with self-alienation among—and discrimination against—the bikers. An entire book could be written about this disreputable but certainly vital genre. Some of the examples with more direct echoes of Wyatt and Billy's adventures include *Little Fauss and Big Halsy* (1970), *C.C. and Company* (1970), *Vanishing Point* (1971), *Werewolves on Wheels* (1971), and, of course, the classic gearhead cycle documentary *On Any Sunday* (1971). *Bunny O'Hare* (1971) should also be mentioned, if only because the motorcycle-riding outlaw "hippies" were here played by the decidedly geriatric Bette Davis and Ernest Borgnine!

Then Came Bronson (1969–1970) was television's *Easy Rider*. It was the story of a San Francisco reporter who, after a friend's suicide, disillusioned with the world he writes about, drops out and climbs aboard a red Harley-Davidson Sportster to travel across America, to New Orleans yet, in search of enlightenment.

Just as "Whaddya got?" distilled the essence of the disaffected biker in the 1950s and "We blew it" did in the 1960s, *Then Came Bronson* hoisted its counterculture flag early in the pilot, when Bronson (played by Michael Parks, a fine actor whose name was often saddled next to the adjective "brooding") pulls up in traffic next to a harried-looking businessman in a suit (played by Stu Klitsner):

Driver: Taking a trip?

Bronson: Yeah.

Driver: Where to?

Bronson: Oh, I don't know. Wherever I end up, I guess.

Driver: Man, I wish I was you.

Bronson: Really?

Driver: Yeah.

Bronson: Well, hang in there.

That pilot aired in March 1969, which means that it actually predated *Easy Rider* by some four months. Something must have been in the air.

In the scramble to attract the Woodstock nation, studios also started making concert films which featured the music of the day. This genre was boosted by, but not created for, the Academy Award–winning documentary *Woodstock* (1970). The actual Woodstock Music Festival was held in mid-August, 1969, while *Easy Rider* was in theaters.

Many movies of the era did not overtly deal with the youth culture or the generation gap, but in an attempt to attract young audiences, flirted with the new permissiveness available since the 1968 MPAA ratings system had brought in Jack Valenti and replaced the old Motion Picture Production Code, which had been wheezing along since 1934. The studios all experimented with releasing X-rated films (one of them, *Midnight Cowboy*, also in 1969, even won a Best Picture Oscar) and amped up the sexuality and alternative lifestyles on-screen in a sometimes-desperate attempt to be hip.

Actually, virtually every film genre was affected by the youth movement, and consequently by *Easy Rider*. There were counterculture war films: *Catch-22* (1970) and *MASH* (1970); horror movies: *Dracula A.D. 1972* (1972) and *The Deathmaster* (1973); the so-called "acid" Westerns: *El Topo* (1970) and *Soldier Blue* (1970); dramas: *Five Easy Pieces* (1970) and *Joe* (1970); romances: *Love Story* (1970) and *Breezy* (1973); comedies: *Brewster McCloud* (1970) and *There's a Girl in My Soup* (1970); and even religious films: *The Cross and the Switchblade* (1970) and *Jesus Christ Superstar* (1972).

It is possible that some of these movies might have been made had *Easy Rider* not existed. But the willingness of Hollywood to tackle counterculture-themed material and to hire people of the counterculture generation, in an attempt to appeal to that generation, can all be traced to that day in Toronto when Peter Fonda picked up a picture of he and Bruce Dern astride motorcycles. Without *Easy Rider*, there would have been no George Lucas, so no *Star Wars*; no Francis Ford Coppola, so no *Godfather*; no Steven Spielberg, no Martin Scorsese, no Brian De Palma—no modern Hollywood. In fact, without the infusion of youth and young blood into the industry, at a time when Hollywood was being run by old men and old ideas, one wonders if the film business as we know it today could have long survived.

In a more-direct way, *Easy Rider* influenced other movies which came after it, either thematically, as above, or by directly or indirectly referencing the movie itself. Certainly, it's impossible to play "Born to

Be Wild" in a movie (or in life) without thinking of Captain America and Billy.

Higher and Higher (1970), a German-Swiss sex and motorcycles saga, was perhaps the first film to reference *Easy Rider*, in the form of a poster seen on a wall. This same "easy" way to evoke the film and its era is also used in numerous other movies of the era, and later eras, some of them exploitation films, some of them pornographic, some mainstream. *Alex in Wonderland* (1970), Paul Mazursky's follow-up to *Bob and Carol and Ted and Alice*, was perhaps the first studio movie to do this. *Rabid* (1977), *Sid and Nancy* (1986), and *Paper Mask* (1990), among many others, followed.

Sleazy Rider (1972) was the first film to parody the film in its title. "Cheesy Rider," "Sneezy Rider," "Uneasy Rider," "Greasy Rider," and "Queasy Rider" have all been utilized as well, usually in television, as an episode title, or internally, in the dialogue.

One of the best of the *Easy Rider* satires is *Lost in America* (1985), which was not a satire of the film itself so much as a satiric look at the film's audience, and what happened when that audience cut their hair and dropped back in. It starred Albert Brooks as an exasperated yuppie who, when he loses his job, avows to drop out of society and travel across the country, *Easy Rider*-style. The joke is that he decides to do it in a monstrous Winnebago, and to take his wife (Julie Hagerty) along. When she loses their savings in Las Vegas, she reassures him that "In *Easy Rider*, the movie you're basing your entire life on, they had no nest egg!"

"They had a giant nest egg. They had all this cocaine!" Brooks screams back.

He proceeds to tell everyone he meets throughout the movie how he is emulating *Easy Rider*, to the bemusement or confusion or delight of the other characters, depending upon their perceptions, or ignorance, of the movie. *Lost in America*'s soundtrack, of course, includes "Born to Be Wild." The joke here is that the self-absorbed Brooks doesn't seem to remember how bad an end the characters in *Easy Rider* eventually came to.

Electra Glide in Blue (1973), *Nashville* (1975), *Race for Your Life, Charlie Brown* (1977), *Repo Man* (1984), *1969* (1988), *Harley-Davidson and the Marlboro Man* (1994), *Pulp Fiction* (1994), *Beavis and Butt-Head*

Do America (1996), *Fear and Loathing in Las Vegas* (1998), *Glass Tiger* (2001), *Starsky and Hutch* (2004), *Borat: Cultural Learnings of America for Make Benefit Glorious Nation of Kazakhstan* (2006), *Crank* (2006), *Mr. Bean's Holiday* (2007), *Loop* (2007), *Hotel for Dogs* (2009), *Rango* (2011), *Paddington* (2014), and *The Boss Baby* (2017) are among the many other movies which somehow found occasion to spoof or reference *Easy Rider*, often through the use of the song "Born to Be Wild." Other references to the movie, such as a callout in the dialogue, or that shot of the poster on a wall, or the innumerable television mentions and spoofs and parodies of the film, again often utilizing "Born to Be Wild," easily tally up into the hundreds.

An even better way to evoke *Easy Rider* on-screen remains convincing one of its stars to make an appearance. Merely seeing Fonda or Hopper in any 1960s-era context has always been enough to conjure up the ghosts of Wyatt and Billy (Jack Nicholson, largely, has been spared this comparison). Occasionally, both actors have taken those ready-made comparisons a step further by overtly evoking the earlier film through dialogue or music (cue up "Born to Be Wild"), or costuming.

Dennis Hopper, certainly, was intentionally exorcising the ghosts of *Easy Rider* in director Wim Wenders's *The American Friend* (1977), in which, as the title character, he comments that "this river reminds me of another river," evoking "The Ballad of Easy Rider," which the actor then sings/quotes from.

Yet another river is evoked by *The River's Edge* (1986), which cast Hopper as a pot-dealing old biker who Winkler says "could well be *Easy Rider*'s Billy gone rotten."[169] *Out of the Blue* (1980) was the first film Hopper directed after *The Last Movie*. He also cast himself as an ex-con biker. *Rumble Fish* (1983) utilized Hopper as the father of an enigmatic character called "Motorcycle Boy." In *Flashback* (1990), Hopper's lifetime hippie tells costar Kiefer Sutherland that "You can't just go to your local video store and rent *Easy Rider* to be a rebel" (and yes, "Born to Be Wild" is used on the soundtrack). Lastly, *Hell Ride* (2008) was an intentionally retro biker flick with Hopper along for, well, the ride.

Peter Fonda, too, has not been above evoking, or even mocking, Captain America over the decades. In 1974 he did a seventeen-minute motorcycle safety film, *Not So Easy*, which began with him pulling up on his motorcycle and saying "Remember me?" In *The Cannonball Run* (1981), Fonda cameos briefly as a biker who wears a black leather jacket rimmed with red, white, and blue. Most surprisingly, his appearance in both of these films was *not* accompanied by "Born to Be Wild."

In *Bodies, Rest & Motion* (1993), Fonda appeared as a biker yet again, this time as a favor to his daughter Bridget, who was the star, and, you may recall, also appeared briefly with her dad in *Easy Rider*.

There's more. *Love and a .44* (1994) featured Captain America's motorcycle's gas tank, with that iconic American flag intact, which it appears has now been transformed into a lamp decorating Fonda's character's apartment. *Ghost Rider* (2007) has Fonda transform Nicholas Cage into a superhero cyclist. In *The Limey* (1999), his character reflects, negatively, about the 1960s, and finally, in *Wild Hogs* (2007), Fonda tells John Travolta and his "gang" of weekend warriors to "lose the watches"— just as Wyatt had tossed his own watch away, at that point, thirty-eight years earlier.

Both of the stars have also appeared in *Easy Rider*–themed advertisements. In the late 1990s, Hopper did a clever Ford Cougar Sports Coupe commercial where the actor is seen driving across the country, accompanied by both "Born to Be Wild" and by his younger self astride his Billy bike. The commercial ends with Hopper driving past Billy, somehow leaving him behind.

Of course, "Born to Be Wild" also accompanies a 2017 Super Bowl commercial in which Peter Fonda's Mercedes-AMG GT Roadster inadvertently blocks in some carousing bikers' hogs at a Route 66 roadhouse. When the gang recognizes who is behind the wheel, they back off in awe. "Still looking good," one of the gang's "old ladies" comments.

For years there was talk of an actual sequel to *Easy Rider* as well. In 1983 Dennis Hopper described to an incredulous reporter his concept for a movie, to be called either *Biker's Heaven* or *Biker Heaven* (sources differ), which, he explained

takes place one hundred years after a nuclear holocaust. This guy comes from outer space and brings Peter and me back to life to save America, which has been overrun by mutant bike gangs, black Nazis, and lesbian sadists. Armed with a magic "don't tread on me" flag, they set out on a mission to find an honest man in the United States and get him elected president. You remember how we got kicked out of the restaurant? Well, this time we go into a restaurant, and there are guys in there with leather and razor blades on their knuckles, and we knock out about fifteen of them. . . . Some things will stay the same. There's some atomic weed, which is more than dynamite stuff.[170]

As much as one wants to think that Hopper was kidding, his story was taken seriously enough by Bert Schneider that he spent, according to Steve Blauner, $100,000 developing the idea. Intriguingly, comic writer and performer Michael O'Donoghue was hired, along with Nelson Lynn, to write the screenplay. "When you have a sequel that begins with two dead protagonists, a rather bold plot line is called for,"[171] O'Donoghue drolly commented to *Rolling Stone* at the time.

Also intriguing was the fact that Terry Southern was involved (understandably, he was incredulous), although it's possible he might have been attached only to prevent him from suing anyone. Michael O'Donoghue and Terry Southern were already friends, and fellow recreational drug users, which didn't stop Southern from exclaiming, "How can they make a sequel when we killed off both the characters?" But nobody was listening. Blauner pulled no punches when he called the script he was finally handed "the worst piece of shit I ever read."[172] *Biker's Heaven* (or, if you prefer, *Biker Heaven*) eventually, finally, went away when Jack Nicholson refused to participate.

In 1987, Columbia Pictures (through their Tri-Star affiliate) announced that *they* were going to make a sequel to *Easy Rider*. Again, both Fonda and Hopper were scheduled, or at least announced, to star, only this time apparently to be cast as entirely different characters. The announcement of this project by the studio might have been only a legal placeholder, and this *Easy Rider* project was not heard from again.

Six years later, in 1993, producer Sheryl Hardy announced yet another, and apparently unrelated, sequel to be called *Easy Rider II*. Details of the plot were not released, but Hardy said that the budget would be between

$8–$10 million, and that, again, Dennis Hopper would direct. Again, this project died quickly and quietly.

In 2000, actor Martin Landau, of all people, proposed a promising *Easy Rider* sequel, to be called *Easy Rider A.D.*, which involved the children of Captain America and George Hanson (who knew?) teaming up to track down the killers of their parents, and inadvertently retracing their journey across America in the process. Another version of the same script now purported that Captain America was actually still alive, but in prison, and that his daughter was now trying to prove him innocent of killing George Hanson! Peter Fonda was briefly attached, and *his* daughter Bridget was courted to play Wyatt's daughter. Bert Schneider partnered with Landau and director Tony Vitale to develop the $30 million project, which, again, apparently never got much past the planning stages.

A sequel to *Easy Rider was* produced, however, but not by Fonda or Hopper, or by anyone mentioned above, or, in fact, by anyone anywhere in Hollywood! What's more, this sequel's existence appears to partially stem from the failure of the two original stars, and Columbia, and Schneider, and Hardy, and Landau, to get their projects produced.

Citing these multiple failures, Phil Pitzer, a wily Cincinnati lawyer, swooped in and bought the sequel rights to *Easy Rider* from Columbia, in partnership with several other investors, around 2003. Bert Schneider, however, immediately sued both Pitzer and Columbia, claiming that he alone, and not the studio, owned the *Easy Rider* sequel rights. The subsequent legal back-and-forth between the studio, and between Pitzer and Schneider, ultimately took four long, remarkably litigious years. And again remarkably, it was the complete Hollywood novice Pitzer who ultimately emerged victorious.

By this time, however, Phil Pitzer seemed to have exhausted the resources with which he had planned to make the movie. At different times over the next six years he claimed that the sequel was ready and awaiting release, but except for some promotional footage, it never materialized. Most of the film appears to have been shot circa 2009. Locations included Acapulco, Ohio, Arizona, California, and South Dakota. Pitzer has claimed through his publicist that the budget was about $10 million. He also claimed in some interviews that Dennis Hopper at one point was interested in directing, before he got sick. The credited director is one Dustin Rikert, who went on to direct another biker flick, the tellingly titled *Born Wild* (2012).

Easy Rider: The Ride Back (also known as *Easy Rider 2: The Ride Home*), "premiered" at a motorcycle festival in Florida (!) in 2012. The following year it was released on DVD. Whether or not it ever played theatrically anywhere, in any legitimate venue, is unknown. The film's distribution was so spotty that few critics were able to find and review the finished film. Those who did were horrified. Leonard Maltin, one of the brave few who sought out the project, called the picture a "staggeringly bad attempt to cash in on the iconic original," and "poor on all counts."[173]

Peter Fonda, whose opinion, of course, holds more weight than any critic, was horrified as well. He told the British Film Institute that "it sucks."[174] About Pitzer, who ended up also playing the lead, and whose name Fonda seemingly could not remember, Fonda said, "I mean, what a fool. And I told him, don't try it. You're going to be stepped on by the critics. You'll never make it. Write your own *Easy Rider*. Find your own stuff today. Don't try to emulate me. There's a phrase, 'Bitch stole my look'; well, he stole my costume, he thought he looked like me, he made a motorcycle like mine. You know, excuse me, you don't do that. That's bad bags!"[175]

Obviously, *Easy Rider: The Ride Back* is a very flawed movie. In his years of stumping to get his movie made and distributed, Phil Pitzer often spoke about how important the original movie was to him, and how it changed his life, so it is good to see that, unlike some sequels, which ignore the continuity of their predecessors when it suits them, this one strives to be an actual continuation of the story, albeit with no original actors or characters. For example, the death of Wyatt's mother is here dramatized, although the film chocks that tragedy up to a completely unmotivated case of postpartum depression!

As the film opens, a voiceover narration recounts: "I had a brother, Wyatt; he had this nickname, Captain America. Day after Mardi Gras, 1969, Wyatt and his best friend Billy were riding their bikes, heading for Florida. The sky was crystal blue. Just like 9/11. Wyatt died that day. The victim of hatred and prejudice. At the hands of those whose greatest fear is freedom, whether in the form of a nation or a single individual." Because this is an officially hard-fought and authorized sequel, the dialogue plays under the actual footage from the original film of Captain America's bike being blown to hell. The character offering this narration is one Morgan Williams, and this is the role played by none other than Phil Pitzer.

Yes, Pitzer dresses himself in Wyatt's Captain America costume and puts himself on Wyatt's Captain America bike (both rebuilt; the black leather jacket even bothers to include Billy's cryptic Defense Department badge) and hits the road.

As amoral as some (just about anybody, actually) might consider it, to compare Wyatt and Billy's fate to 9/11, and as kneejerk as it is to blame those rednecks with shotguns in the first movie for fearing national or individual freedoms, to be fair, this opening is, for *Easy Rider* fans, *exactly* what could be desired from a movie which has the nerve to call itself (sometimes) *Easy Rider 2*. Somebody gets on a chopper, guns it, and rides away. Hell, yes.

Pitzer, at least sometimes, does bear an uncanny resemblance to Peter Fonda in his black leathers. He teams up with another biker named "Wes Coast," played by Jeff Fahey, and they head north at the behest of his sister (and Wes's old flame), Shane, who is played by coproducer Sheree J. Wilson, to visit Morgan's dying father (Newell Alexander).

It seems that Wyatt left behind a whole family filled with troubled relationships, all of them sporting names that evoke Western legends. His nephew is named Cody, his father is Wild Bill, and he has yet another brother named Virgil. Never mind that Peter Fonda always wanted Captain America to be a rootless cypher. Here, we are told that Captain America had a last name as well, Williams. Captain America is Wyatt Williams.

The footage of Morgan and Wes on their road odyssey *is* beautiful, with lots of László Kovács–inspired vistas and sunsets (no lens flares, though), and Pitzer and Fahey evoke, as they should, Captain America and Billy. (There are also more helicopter shots than the first movie was able to afford, which is a plus.) On the road, they help out an old friend who is feeding the homeless from a school bus by giving him their money (Morgan has a stash of drug cash hidden—where else?—in his gas tank). They get drunk in a colorful biker roadhouse, buy some reefer ("Around here, we call it pot," a blonde chopper chick, young enough to be their granddaughter, helpfully informs them), and camp out, smoking that pot and conversing about life in the evenings, *Easy Rider* style. Morgan also visits the Salton Sea, eyeballs a decomposing fish, and is made to say "We've really blown it, man. We've gotta start taking better care of the planet."

These scenes obviously were designed to mimic those in the earlier film, which they do well enough; however, there is no consideration of the fact that forty-plus years have passed. (It's torturously hard to pin down exactly what year the movie is set, due, no doubt, to the endless production schedule.) Why, for example, do Morgan and Wes camp out? Motels *still* don't allow hippies? And aren't there helmet laws in effect in some states in the twenty-first century? (Dittoing the iconography of the original, Wes doesn't seem to own a helmet; Morgan does, complete with the Stars and Stripes, but he never wears it.)

Also, the music which plays under these scenes, as can be imagined, is not as brilliantly inspired as in the original. In fact, the selection of songs, which includes, believe it or not, those counterculture classics "America, the Beautiful," and "Amazing Grace," are mostly droned in an easy-listening, soft-rock/country patois, which Wyatt and Billy would have laughed at.

Still, the road-trip sequences in *Easy Rider: The Ride Back* do achieve a sort of lyricism, manufactured to order though they may be. It's the rest of the film that goes horribly wrong.

It seems that the Williams family, while they wait for Wild Bill to die, and for Morgan to come ambling back home, is prone to reminiscing about itself. They do this a lot. Via lots and lots of flashbacks. It's hard to be sure, but there are possibly flashbacks *within* flashbacks. And there are flashbacks by people who were not there to have experienced what is being flash-backed to. The movie includes flashbacks of characters fighting in World War II, and then flashbacks of these characters fighting their devils, postwar. Flashbacks to Vietnam, likewise, are included, as are flashbacks of that war's home-front protests and aftermath. Most disturbingly, young Virgil Williams (Chris Engen), again in flashback, falls in love with a rich girl (her snobbish parents—surprise—object to their daughter's cycle-riding boyfriend), and they are both subsequently attacked and brutally raped by "bad" bikers—in another flashback.

Pitzer apparently has a military background, and his affection for veterans is obvious and undoubtedly sincere. (In 2015 he released a special "military edition" of his movie to support disabled veterans.) But that pro-military bias, if it can be called that, is entirely at odds with the pacifist counterculture philosophy behind *Easy Rider*. "You can attack the war, man, but never the warrior," he says, as Morgan. Here Pitzer seems to be trying to justify the conservative bias of a movie which he has grafted onto another movie, which sports a viewpoint much further to the left. At least the use of the word "man" is authentic.

Viewers have always been able to take out of *Easy Rider* whatever they put into it. Fonda and Hopper's superficial relationship with the "freaks," and their rather unfocused protest against the "straights," has long given their film an unintended and liquid appeal to both liberals, who perhaps appreciate its quasi-socialist posturings, and conservatives, who feel that the film is actually telling the government to stop persecuting our cowboys and overregulating our citizens.

J. F. X. Gillis, a blogger for *Newsvine*, thinks that the conservative message in the original *Easy Rider* is actually even more overt. He said in 2010 that "if this narrative had been medieval, could there be any doubt at all of the theme, or the moral teaching intended? Sinners wander the countryside on a secular quest, encountering God's message but failing to acknowledge Him."[176]

Even further to the right, Fonda has joked about how, in the Deep South, when Captain America and Billy are blown away, some audiences cheered in approval!

It would be fascinating to see what emotions Peter Fonda look-alike Phil Pitzer took away from that movie back in 1969.

Whatever political leanings one has, however, *Easy Rider: The Ride Back* is a frustrating experience. As mentioned, the cinematography by Brian Lataille is beautiful, and succeeds in making one pine for the joys of the open road. The production values are better than they apparently have any right to be, considering the chaotic nature of the shoot. But the film ultimately pulls itself apart due to the woefully unfocused and cluttered script (by Pitzer and Rikert), and the acting.

Almost surprisingly, not all of that acting works against *Easy Rider: The Ride Back*. Veteran actor Jeff Fahey steals the film; his rascally old biker with a bad-boy gleam in his eyes is what one might imagine Billy might have turned into had he not driven south after Mardi Gras. TV veteran Sheree J. Wilson is more than capable as Shane. One imagines her coproducing the film partially to give herself a showcase as an actress, and she succeeds. Michael Nouri and beloved character actor Rance Howard are among the only other recognizable actors in the cast, although baseball legend Johnny Bench shows up briefly as a major league scout (speculation has suggested that perhaps Pitzer, who had once been his lawyer, was still owed a favor).

Phil Pitzer took most—well, all—of the critical brickbats for his turn as Morgan. Online reviewer Paul Mavis scoffed at *DVD Talk* that "had first-time actor Pitzer been merely hired for this job, you could simply chalk up his unintentionally amusing parody of Fonda to bad acting. However, the difference between a jobbing actor blowing a role and a novice with a wad of cash giving himself the lead role in his own self-financed movie is altogether two different things: one's a poor actor, and the other is a wannabe starring in his own vanity project."[177]

Film and music critic Nathan Rabin, over at *The Dissolve*, called Pitzer "a strange-looking man on the wrong side of 60 who looks like a cross between a blurry Peter Fonda and a slender leather recliner . . . Pitzer favors sleeveless T-shirts, bandannas, and leather pants, as befits a man who's spent the previous four decades selling weed, designing awesome jewelry, and having sex with beautiful naked women young enough to be his granddaughters."[178]

It should be noted that other Internet reviews have been less forgiving than the above.

Easy Rider: The Ride Back's official website, which does not appear to have been updated since 2015, states that "Over the last six years, Philip Pitzer has become involved in motion picture development focusing exclusively on the *Easy Rider* franchise. Mr. Pitzer has coauthored two scripts, *Easy Rider: The Ride Back* and *Easy Rider: The Search Continues*,"[179] which indicates that a third episode in the "trilogy" may be on the way.

Let's hope the next one is an easier ride.

Easy Rider—the original, that is—has survived the 1960s, the counterculture that spawned it, and the Vietnam war it avoided; it has outdistanced in popular culture many other films more critically praised in 1969. *Midnight Cowboy* won the Best Picture Oscar that year. It's a good movie, to be sure, but when was the last time it was parodied in a Super Bowl ad? Hopefully, no one has ever tried to live their lives based on *Midnight Cowboy*'s slimy Ratso Rizzo character, either.

Easy Rider has also outlived much of its own rhetoric. The 1960s unofficially ended in December 1969 at the Altamont Free Concert in Northern California, when spectator Meredith Hunter was stabbed by Hells Angel Alan Passaro, and three other people eventually died. Later, movies like *The Big Fix* (1978), *The Return of the Secaucus 7* (1980), and *The Big Chill* (1983) examined the survivors of the 1960s from the perspective of the 1970s and '80s, and discovered that a lot of Billys and Wyatts had cut their hair and tarped their choppers and dropped back in.

"The American hippie, which has since gone on to become an archetype every bit as enduring and powerful as say, the American cowboy, had never really received that kind of iconic treatment before,"[180] Joel Selvin of the *San Francisco Chronicle* remarked in 2009 about *Easy Rider*'s "encapsulating of a moment, and a movement, which, as the years separated us from the trappings of that era, perhaps made those accoutrements appear increasingly quaint, even to those that were there."[181]

The film itself is so much a part of its time that unlike at least some other "classic" movies, it is hard to separate it from that time. Today, nostalgia has burnished the appeal of *Easy Rider*, even among those who were not around to remember that era firsthand. In fact, part of the movie's ironically timeless appeal is the very alienness of some of its costumes and attitudes. Watching the film and traveling across America with Captain America and Billy in the twenty-first century is as exotic and whimsical as navigating the Mississippi with Huck and Jim. One wants to do it, even if it has been rendered unrelatable by time, even to the now-aging baby boomers who originally wanted to do it, and for whom the film was made.

There is no more surefire way to prove that something has gone into the cultural lexicon than when it is name-dropped by the president, or by a future president. During the 1988 presidential campaign, George Bush evoked the film by name, and what he called "the *Easy Rider* Society," and not favorably either. "Some of the young people in college today probably don't believe this, but people used to talk like those movies of the '60s," he said condescendingly. "They thought drug use was 'cool,' and advised you to 'Do your own thing.'" Bush claimed that the country had gone from the 1960s *Easy Rider* era—"Go ahead, have a nice weekend"—to Clint Eastwood's more assertive and manly "Go ahead, make my day."[182] And he seemed to think that this was a good thing, too. George Bush also illustrated how the film was now seen as part of an era that had passed by.

The film's twenty-fifth anniversary in 1994 included retrospective screenings of the movie, media events, and, on July 18, a party at Thunder Roadhouse, a restaurant on the Sunset Strip in West Hollywood, co-owned, aptly, by Fonda and Hopper.

Seeing the movie again that year, Roger Ebert, who had raved about *Easy Rider*'s greatness as a young critic, at the age of fifty-two was now more cynical. About the film he remarked, "[It] was like entering a time machine. It provided all sorts of little shocks of recognition, as when you realize they aren't playing 'Don't Bogart That Joint' for laughs."[183]

Perhaps significantly, about the same time (1995), Ebert also happened to look up his old review of that *other* quintessential film of the 1960s, *Woodstock* (ironically released in March 1970). He then remembered that he had opened *that* review with a quote by 1960s radical Abbie Hoffman, who at the Chicago Seven trial had told the judge that "he was a resident of the Woodstock Nation." Hoffman then proclaimed, about that Woodstock Nation, that "we carry it around with us as a state of mind, in the same way the Sioux Indians carry the Sioux Nation with them." Ebert wrote, when looking at that old clipping, "And look what happened to the Sioux."[184]

The following year, Dennis Hopper was invited to Prague, of all places, where twenty-six years after being banned in Czechoslovakia,

Easy Rider, which had been an underground success among that nation's repressed youth, was finally, officially, released, with Hopper being given a hero's welcome and leading a 150-bike parade to the theater. Czech Republic president Vaclav Havel attended the premiere.

Easy Rider has been commemorated and paid tribute to in myriad, sometimes unexpected ways over the decades. Perhaps the most unusual tribute anywhere to the memories of Wyatt and Billy, however, is to be found in the last place in the world one would expect to find it: Morganza, Louisiana.

We'll let Donnie "Hair Bear" Derbes, who, as a movie-and-motorbike-struck thirteen-year-old, had hung out with the crew in 1968, catch us up as to life in Morganza, and how he ultimately turned out to be instrumental in getting a plaque placed to celebrate the spot where his town had once, uneasily, rubbed shoulders with the counterculture.

Easy Rider, *looking back, was a very big event for my little town. And even after it was all over, after they had all left town, everyone was still talking about it. In the months after, everyone was still going on about what had happened over at Melancon's Café.*

A little over a year after the filming, the movie finally came out. I remember that most of the townsfolk, they didn't like it a bit. They said that it was all about smoking dope, and that they were just making fun of us Southerners. But to me, it was a proud moment in my life. Our little town had been in a movie!

A few years later, in 1971, Easy Rider *was knocked out of the local limelight anyway when, down the road in McCrea, they held a big rock concert—A Celebration of Life, they called it; the whole parish was invaded by outsiders. That event, for many, outdid* Easy Rider.

As for me, I moved away from Morganza for a few years. When I'd tell someone where I was from, they'd bring up the movie and ask, jokingly, if they would be beat up if they went to my hometown, just like what happened to Jack Nicholson in Easy Rider! *I'd play along, and tell them that they wouldn't make it to the parish line—a phrase from the movie!*

I still can't believe how many people know about that movie. I was, and still am, very proud of the locals that were in the movie. Easy Rider has made an impact around the world, and Morganza sure did have a part in that.

Sadly, by the 1980s, Melancon's Café was falling apart. And in 1985, it was finally torn down. Morganza has a very proud history. And in a lot of ways, Melancon's Café was the center of the community. When they tore down Melancon's, it broke my heart.

In 2009, a biker group called LA Riders contacted me. They were trying to get in touch with the girls and with the sheriff who were in the movie. They wanted to get their input about being in the movie.

I set up a meeting with them at the Bears Den, and that's when the wheels started turning. I got the Morganza Historical Society involved, and together, we organized an event that started out at the New Roads Louisiana Museum, where we watched the movie. Then we all rode out to Morganza, to the Bears Den, where we had food and live music.

Out of that event we raised a couple of thousand dollars for the plaque that's now in front of where Melancon's Café once stood. It commemorates Easy Rider, and Morganza's involvement with the film. We had another event the next year, in 2010, to dedicate the plaque, and it was set in place a few days later. Over three hundred people attended the ceremony.

The plaque still stands, and to this day, bikers go on a pilgrimage there to take pictures of the site.[185]

For the 2019 fiftieth anniversary of *Easy Rider*, the Morganza Cultural District erected a full-size painted facade depicting Melancon's Café on the original site, with both the local and visiting stars depicted in the windows, looking out together into a different world.

In the decades since its release, *Easy Rider* has managed to be embraced, and rejected, and embraced again by what remains of the counterculture. It has also been accepted by everyone else. No one finds *Easy Rider* "dangerous" or "rule-breaking" today. A double-barreled indication of its acceptance in the mainstream came in 1998 when the

National Film Registry, as it had done every year since 1988, selected *Easy Rider* as one of twenty-five movies that year which they considered to be "culturally, historically, or aesthetically important." That same year the American Film Institute selected the film as number eighty-eight of the top one hundred American films.

The soundtrack has also continued to sell as the decades have ticked by. In fact, the *Easy Rider* album has become something of a sampler album of the best of the 1960s, for those who were there and remember, those who were there and don't (but pretend they do), and those who weren't born yet. Surprisingly, the album eventually went out of print—not because it was no longer selling, but because it was selling too well, year after year, and the artists were no longer happy about whatever deals their agents had signed in 1969. Obviously, this failure of the power of music over the power of money signified, better than anything else, how long-gone is the era the music celebrates.

In 2000, MCA managed to renegotiate with all of the original artists, or their lawyers, or heirs, including Capitol, and The Band, and a new album, this time on CD, was issued, which contains the original songs, sound effects from the movie, and, as an option, a second disc which contains incidental music and other songs from the era.

It still sounds good.

CHAPTER FIVE

Road Tales

EASY RIDER, AS HAS BEEN SHOWN, HAD A SEISMIC IMPACT ON HOLLYWOOD, as well as its creators and exploiters and benefactors. But the film affected the world outside of Hollywood, too. *Easy Rider*'s ripple effect throughout popular culture is, in fact, unprecedented.

To be fair, all art, by its very nature, is designed to influence its audience to some degree. Since the beginning of civilization man has been banning paintings and burning books and crying at the opera and laughing at the circus and screaming at the stadium and worshipping stars at the movies. That's how it's supposed to work.

But only very rarely does it go beyond that.

The truth is that, sure, *Easy Rider* did, in 1969, reflect what was going on within the population, certainly to a specific segment of it, anyway. Toni Basil, for example, pointed out in 2002 that *Easy Rider* "was the first time that the long-haired guys were the heroes and the short-haired guys were the villains."[186] This was Peter Fonda's intention. He once told Dave Nichols, the editor of *Easyriders* magazine, that "he felt that the Woodstock generation had plenty of passion, and its art included noted poetry and music, but that it lacked a movie that stood as its anthem. Fonda gave a whole generation its anthem with *Easy Rider*."[187]

While Fonda's statement is a bit grandiose, it also undersells the power of *Easy Rider*. The Woodstock Nation, as we know, did not long survive the 1960s. So, if *Easy Rider*'s appeal had been limited purely to the counterculture, that appeal would have dimmed with the memories of those baby boomers who tuned in and dropped out, a demographic that is getting increasingly smaller and grayer as the era recedes. Indeed, as noted, the movie does have the whiff of a museum piece about it, which is how many mainstream critics and viewers will now see it, if they bother to see it at all.

Peter L. Winkler, for example, has said that "with its counterculture elements now passé, *Easy Rider* comes off as little more than a picturesque movie scored with an album of golden oldies."[188]

Sean Macaulay, a critic for the *Daily Beast*, has gotten annoyed at people calling the film "allegorical." In the *London Times* in 1999, he asked, "What is the film allegorical of? It can't be symbolic of a man looking for America. It's clearly about a man looking for America. It's like saying *Midnight Cowboy* is an allegory about unlikely friendship."[189]

Keith Uhlich in *Time Out New York* was even more dismissive of *Easy Rider* in 2010, saying, "a film important to and influential in the flower-power late '60s, *Easy Rider* now seems like a narcissistic hodgepodge of travelogue and passion play."[190]

James L. Neibaur, in a 2017 biography of Jack Nicholson, said that in the twenty-first century, "much of the attitude appeared dated, and hardly presents itself as progressive or open-minded, as it might have seemed to younger people as far back as 1969."[191]

William Bayer, in a 1989 Hollywood how-to book pitched toward would-be filmmakers, took an even more cynical tact. "*Easy Rider*," he says, "fulfilled a craving by a particular segment of the audience (alienated young Americans) for a certain way of life (free, cool, and adventurous) and, at the same time, articulated an apprehension about America (that it is evil), which had not previously been articulated on film." Bayer then goes on to claim that once that craving had been sated, then the perceived "*Easy Rider* audience" would just move on to graze somewhere else, which largely proved to be true."[192]

Even some of those involved in the movie have been critical of its artistic merits. "I didn't care for it very much. I thought it was kind of a hack job. I thought it was compromised, everything was compromised," Robert Walker has said.[193] Although he does admit to warming up to it a bit in subsequent decades.

Yet, against all odds or reason, *Easy Rider* has escaped becoming more than just a relic of a cultural movement which is over, and in fact, which ultimately failed anyway. Somehow, in the early 1970s, and ever since, people have created their own cultural movement, a movement inspired by, yet not exactly based on, the movie.

It should be noted that this "cult" of *Easy Rider* is pretty much unprecedented in popular culture. *The Rocky Horror Picture Show* (1975), for example, has thousands of fans who still go to midnight screenings of their favorite movie dressed in costumes inspired by that movie, but they take those costumes off at 1:40 a.m. when the theater lights come up. For *Easy Rider*, however, the lifestyle continues, Route 66–like, mile after mile, across the landscape of its most devoted fans' entire lives. *Easy Rider*, it seems, has been the primary cause for countless Captain Americas to buy their first motorcycles and to adapt their lifestyles and identities into that biker culture—and in many cases, to never look back.

"There are so many people around the world who come up to me and tell me that *Easy Rider* changed their lives. Most of the long-distance riders I meet tell me that I started the whole thing. I didn't start it at all. I just put it on film," Peter Fonda said in his autobiography in 1998.[194]

To his credit, Fonda apparently is pleased to be a founding father of this brotherhood. Dave Nichols recalls at least one instance of Fonda practicing this philosophy:

A few years ago, I was with Peter Fonda when a grizzled biker walked up, shook his hand, and said, "You changed my life, man. You are the reason I ride."

Peter stood and talked to the biker for over a half an hour. They talked about bikes they had owned, runs that they love to go on, and their favorite places to ride. At the end of their time together, they exchanged hugs like old friends—such is the power of the biker brotherhood.

Afterward, I told Peter that I thought he was extraordinarily kind to give the biker, a complete stranger, so much time. Peter smiled and said, "Dig, man, he has been waiting over thirty-five years to tell me that. Riding is his life. Of course, I gave him my time; that's what it's all about.[195]

Easy Rider moved biker culture beyond the Marlon Brando–inspired "1-percenter" perception that most people then had of cyclists. In contrast to the typical biker characterization in earlier movies, as "daughter-raping, village-pillaging Huns,"[196] as Nichols succinctly puts it, Captain America in *Easy Rider* was thoughtful and introspective. And damn, was he ever cool. Even Billy, who seems to represent the wilder, more hedonistic side of the frontier, is ultimately questing, well-meaning, and loyal to his friend.

Young people in particular in the 1970s found this alternate characterization of bikers, and of this particular biker lifestyle, to be tremendously appealing. For a young man, then as now, the idea of climbing aboard a sexy and powerful chopped cycle and then telling the world, and parents, and college, and the draft board, and the old lady, to all just go to hell—accompanied by a Steppenwolf song and your best friend—was, yeah, tremendously, cosmically, satisfying. Still is.

So, if these young people decided that they wanted a Billy bike, or, more likely, a Captain America bike, in order to make this dream happen, then where to look?

At the time, Harley-Davidson, the obvious place, sold nothing that looked like either bike in *Easy Rider*. A little investigation would reveal to these aspiring bikers that these bikes, these choppers, were not manufactured at all, but adapted from existing machines, crafted individually by hand, by wizard artisans, whose methods were mysterious and hallowed, and whose results were magic.

Most of these choppers seemed to come out of California, out of Watts and San Bernardino. One of the most famous places where this alchemy was performed seemed to be the legendary Denver's Choppers, which had opened in San Bernardino in 1967. "Denver" was Denver Mullins, and he and his partner, Mondo Porras, created what would come to be known as the long "Swedish style," motorcycles apparently so-named because regulations prohibiting such modifications allegedly didn't apply in Sweden. Nevertheless, the style, characterized by a long-raked fork, was invented by Denver, right there in his shop. And today there is actually a cycle club called The Swedish Style—in Sweden.

In 1969 *Easy Rider* came out, "and people started coming into the shop asking for 'Captain America' bikes," Mondo remembers. "In particular, I built one that was an *exact* copy; it went to a guy in Texas."[197]

Other exact (or exact-enough) copies still attract attention on highways all over the world. For example, Graham Gamble of the UK owns a replica Captain America designed by custom-parts specialist Paughco in Carson City, Nevada, and imported to England in 2005. Peter Fonda himself rode Gamble's replica in 2009, and is quoted as saying that "I had a blast." [198] Gamble believes that his bike is one of only two on the continent. "I'd love to go to France and do some serious miles on it," he says. "I want to prove people wrong when they say it's just a pose-mobile."[199]

None of this went unnoticed. In 1971, Harley-Davidson (who you may remember had refused to donate motorcycles for the production of *Easy Rider*) had apparently now seen the desire among enthusiasts for a chopped bike, so they introduced the 74ci FX Super-Glide, the closest thing to a chopper a rider could purchase from the manufacturer. It was painted, significantly, red, white, and blue, and it gave potential Captain Americas, ones who did not have access to a Denver Mullins or a Benny Hardy, the chance to follow the sun themselves.

These potential Captain Americas would have first read about the Super-Glide in a new magazine devoted to their motorcycle lifestyle, called, significantly enough, *Easyriders*. It was created in 1970 by Mil Blair and Joe Teresi, who together talked publisher Lou Kimzey into creating a motorcycle "lifestyle" magazine. There were already motorcycle magazines on newsstands at the time, of course, but they tended to showcase the bikes over the people who built them. *Easyriders*, on the other hand, from the first, was a magazine for the *Easy Rider* generation. Each issue included girls in various stages of undress, draped over motorcycles, of course; cartoons (mostly by Hal Robinson); columns and essays; and, in particular, legendary (among the readers) motorcycle-themed artwork. The magazine also tirelessly battled what it considered unjust regulations regarding choppers, and likewise, laws which they felt restricted bikers' individual rights and freedoms. *Easyriders* was an instantaneous international success, and remains a beloved fixture in the motorcycle community today.

Easyriders, as has been pointed out, also sounds suspiciously like *Easy Rider*. Dave Nichols, the twenty-year (and counting) editor of the magazine, who had his life changed when he talked his parents into taking him to see *Easy Rider* in the theater when he was a kid, eventually met Peter Fonda, who he says initially "had a burr in his saddle" about his movie's title being shanghaied. "Today he loves us. He found out how much good we were doing for the biker community, and for his movie."[200]

That community, the one that *Easy Rider* created, includes a lot of people who, like Dave Nichols, saw the movie, either theatrically, or in one of its hundreds of subsequent television and reissue and home-video screenings, and often at an impressionable age, and consequently can trace their subsequent interest in motorcycles, and in the *Easyriders* lifestyle, to the film. It's hard to find a motorcyclist, or motorcycle enthusiast, of any age who has not been influenced by the movie, even, as is probably the case with many younger riders, inadvertently.

Many modern motorcyclists, to be sure, got into biking not because they saw *Easy Rider*, but because they saw and met and were influenced by riders who had gotten into biking because *they* saw *Easy Rider*. The original influence might be several generations old now, but the DNA is intact. Even after fifty years on the road.

Many fans bought their first motorcycle, or begged their parents to buy it for them, directly because of *Easy Rider*. This first motorcycle might have been a Honda rather than a Harley, but the feeling of personal freedom—and of the freedom of the open road that the movie imparts so vividly—was the same. And they carry this adrenaline rush, this king-of-the-road high, throughout their lives, whether they are weekend warriors who strip off their leathers and wash the dirt from under their fingernails on Sunday nights, or grizzled 1-percenters, old lions who have pledged their lives to the lifestyle.

Easyriders does not have a monopoly on the attention of these very diverse motorcyclists. *Motorcyclist, Biker Babes, Born to Ride, Old School Biker, Chopper, Outlaw Biker,* and *Supercycle* are just a sampling of other titles. Many more can be found online as fanzines or e-magazines. All of them share *Easy Rider* as an inspiration and a totem. The editor of one of these magazines, *100% Biker*, which is published thirteen times a year (!) in the United Kingdom, is Blue Miller, who shares his thoughts here about *Easy Rider*.

When all is said and done, it's just a film. Actors playing made-up characters in a made-up story and, for that matter, not even likable characters. And yet, when I look back, Easy Rider *has haunted so many areas of my life, always there in the corner of my eye.*

It's not a film with which I've had an easy relationship. I initially came to Easy Rider *with a peculiarly British attitude. As a student, perhaps my reading on it was a little removed from the traditional "hippies seeking the American dream" theme. At the time I was studying at a university well-known for its demonstrations and radical politics, and, from that perspective, I was well placed to see* Easy Rider *as a class allegory, the class system being far more ingrained in British culture than in that of America.*

From the start, Wyatt and Billy are doomed. They make their money by a cocaine deal, cocaine being at the time the drug of the upper classes; two guys taking money off a toff—Phil Spector in his flash car—and that would never do. Here, being turned away from the Pine Breeze Inn is not so much anti-hippie or anti-biker as a reminder of the notices prevalent in the rented accommodation of UK towns which had so recently stated "No Blacks. No Irish. No Dogs." George Hanson, the educated lawyer, is punished for the sin of associating with those outside his class with the ultimate penalty. And, of course, Wyatt and Billy can't be seen to be getting above their station, of succeeding, even in the blue-collar dream of retiring to Florida.

That's one reading, but remember, I was a teenager then. Later, some of my early idealism kicked out of me by real life, I came back to Easy Rider *a part of motorcycling culture. But the bikers that I knew who idolized the film hated the hippie culture. In many ways, they had more in common with the rednecks in the truck than Wyatt and Billy on motorcycles, much as they wanted long forks and tiny fuel tanks on their Honda CB750s. They saw the choppers and the long straight roads and nothing else. If anything, for many, Lázlo Kovács's cinematography was the most influential part of this film, instilling in so many the desire to ride those same roads (and for me, as a film student [with] an appreciation of photographic technique, it was a movie I dissected for my studies). Can it be coincidence that [those from the] generation who grew up watching* Easy Rider *are now those signing up for motorcycle tours of Route 66 to celebrate their fiftieth or sixtieth birthdays?*

Which brings me to Route 66, which became, after a few initial trips, a new love for me. Back on those early journeys I didn't know that Easy Rider *had used Route 66 as a backdrop for the first half of the film. When I found out that those roads I'd been traveling through—Needles, Flagstaff, and Las Vegas, Nevada—were the ones that had taken Fonda and Hopper eastwards, it was as if the film had tapped me on the shoulder and said "Still here . . ."*

And then, there's what I do for a living. Over the last twenty years I have edited three of the top custom motorcycle magazines in Europe, yes, custom motorcycles, just like the "Captain America" Panhead. Easy Rider *isn't the reason that I do the job I do, at least not in the sense of a blinding flash of revelation. I didn't see the film and instantly decide on this career path. However, without* Easy Rider, *the whole custom motorcycle industry might have taken a very different direction, one that wouldn't have led me to where I am now.*

But after all, it's just a film.[201]

Daryl "Caveman" Nelson is a professed "outcast" biker who always longed to ride, like Wyatt and Billy, across Monument Valley. He did, but the journey took him forty years . . .

Rolling to a stop just past the guardrail onto a little plateau overlooking the valley below, the famous mesas stood timelessly, observing the lives that passed by. Time has a way of dissipating in this unchanging landscape. Billy and Wyatt could have ridden by just moments ago.

I slid out the stand and leaned my chop over. The 21 Avon slid just a bit in the dirt from the 14-inch over-raked forks, making the pebbles underneath grind in protest. Patting the coffin tank as I dismounted, the sense of peace caught me by surprise in its intensity. I had finally completed a lifelong dream: I had ridden my custom hardtail through Monument Valley!

It was forty years earlier, almost to the day, that a ten-year-old "outcast" had sat down on the rug in front of the old Zenith to watch the 9:00 movie of the week. TV Guide had only described it as "Easy Rider; two bikers on a journey to find America."

Two hours later, my life had been irrevocably changed. I already knew that Captain America's chariot was the most amazing piece of rolling chrome I had ever seen. And I also knew that whatever it took, I was gonna have one of my own someday.

What I didn't realize—not yet—was that Easy Rider *had shown me a way forward in life.*

The word biker *did not have much meaning to a kid in southwestern Massachusetts. Motorcycles passed by our house only a few times a week. But I loved the sound they made and already hoped, someday, to have my own. However, I had never seen or heard of this creation I saw in the movie, called a chopper. There weren't a lot of them in rural New England during the early seventies.*

At the time, being a social outcast due to a speech impediment and severe hearing loss, I never quite fit in anywhere. In my young worldview, everyone in society was just like the rednecks in the diner scene. I thought then that I was always going to have to go it alone. Easy Rider *showed me, for the first time, that other "outcasts" were out there.*

Every person in life, even if they don't realize it, is looking for adventure. Motorcycles, as Wyatt showed, could be a path to finding it. Truer concepts have rarely been captured on film.

I was thinking about all of this as I threw a leg over and forcefully jumped the kick-start. The twin roared alive. Kicking her into first and releasing the clutch shot gravel over the edge of the overlook. I pointed my own five-spoke invader west towards Sedona, and then on to Oak Creek Canyon, which was the destination.

On the way, other scenes played in my mind's eye, looking at the river's clear water flowing across the flat rocks, I began to realize that the personal journey of my life had been set in motion, largely, by Easy Rider.

In the forty years since being inspired by the movie, I have ridden through most of the US, Canada, and Mexico; met brothers and sisters on two wheels from the world over; [ridden] with Dan Haggerty, who was in the movie and owned the actual "Captain America" bike. I have also ridden with, and come to call brother or sister, famous and infamous bikers from the world over. I also became, for a time, part of a biker organization that helped rescue abused children from harm, and I'm proud to have played a part in the raising of many thousands of dollars for various noteworthy causes. This movie has also inspired me to become a writer of biker fiction, based on my own adventures.

And all this came from a low-budget, counterculture, independent film, a film destined to change the world.

Thanks, Wyatt and Billy.[202]

Like many fans of the movie, and the lifestyle, Randy Beckstrand's memories of *Easy Rider* are also tied to his childhood, and his father:

Back in around 1970, my dad was taking a psychology class at Long Beach State University. As part of an assignment he did a report on the movie Easy Rider. *So, we all went to see the movie. I vaguely remember being in the back of a car at a drive-in movie—and seeing a man with an American flag on his helmet and on his motorcycle.*

The whole time I was growing up, that memory, that image, kept coming back to my mind on a regular basis. Especially when I was around motorcycles.

My dad's family had a machine shop in Long Beach, and most of my dad's family and many of his friends worked there. Back in those days we had a sort of ritual that when you worked at the shop, you got to, regularly, with the other family and staff there, go out for long motorcycle rides. So, we got to ride all over Southern California and beyond. Frazier Park, Ventura Highway, and to Buellton, to a place called Anderson's, for pea soup. All of these were favorite destinations for these rides.

My dad's family mainly rode Moto Guzzis, because my dad's cousin had a Moto Guzzi dealership, and he got them good deals, but there was also the occasional Harley, BMW, Ducati, Yamaha, and Kawasaki. Everyone in the family in those days used to ride, so I grew up on the back of my dad's bike, touring Southern California.

Fast-forward to 1989. I was living in my aunt's driveway in a camper-trailer with my friend Alan, and we were mowing lawns for a living. If I remember right, we got to talking about motorcycles one day, but all we could afford to do was go to the video store. While there, we both saw the video box for Easy Rider. *I recognized from the artwork on the cover that American flag helmet and motorcycle from when I was three or four years old. So we took the movie and watched it over at my grandpa's house.*

We were hooked! The freedom of Captain America and Billy on the open road, as shown in the film, along with the music, was exactly what we were craving.

We decided we needed to ride. I ended up with a BMW R75/5, and Alan bought a Honda Magna. We rode all around LA and up into the mountains, too, on many a night ride. Looking back on those days and on those rides, it was just like in the movie. It was just like when I was a kid, with my dad. It was pure freedom.

My feeling about the movie Easy Rider *is that it is the best depiction of that pure freedom—of being on the open road, on a bike, with your buddy, that any movie has ever given us. And that music; it's perfect and it's inspiring, as is the scenery. And those bikes are a dream.*

It's not always a good dream, though. The depiction in the movie of the realities of a biker's life on the road, although a bit clichéd and overdone, are realistically stark and in-your-face. Like I said, being on a bike can be the best and freest feeling in the world, but if you go down, or if someone wants to take you out, it can be very unforgiving, just as the ending of the movie shows. I hate this part. But this sort of thing will always be a possibility every time you throw your leg over your bike and hit the road.

Even so, I've already called my dad and made plans to have him help get my Guzzi back on the road this spring so we can hit the road again.

Thankfully, he's still game. And so am I.[203]

Tom Elliot is a cyclist who has had his share, over many long rides, of *Easy Rider* moments:

My name is Tom. I started my two-wheeled adventures with a mini-bike. I was fourteen.

Two years later, in 1969, I saw Easy Rider *in the theater. I was instantly hooked!*

I moved up to a 175 Honda the next year, and on to a bigger 450 Honda after that, which I promptly customized into an Easy Rider*–inspired "chopper"-style machine. It had a big fat rear tire, a two-tiered seat with sissy bar, chrome megaphone pipes, extended front end, custom headlight, and high handlebars!*

At first, I just went on local rides with my high school buddies. Then I took some longer weekend road trips. I'll never forget the first one, where we biked over to Ludington, Wisconsin. After riding the hundred miles to get over there, we found a field. We lit a joint, and we cranked up the Steppenwolf and other '60s hit tunes. We had an unforgettable Easy Rider *night out there under the stars.*

After that bike got stolen back in 1979, I was off the road for thirty-five years. But five years ago, I got back into riding. My driver's license still had a cycle endorsement on it after all those years! This time, I bought a V4 Honda Magna, which is kind of a chopper-looking bike, only this time, right out of the factory.

I've stuck with the V4s since then, and have ridden almost one hundred thousand miles, most of them on my current Honda, an ST 1300, which, like me, now has over a hundred thousand miles on it.

I'm proud to have now completed four of the very well-named "Iron Butt Saddle Sore 1,000" rides, which certify that a rider has undertaken a one-thousand-mile ride, one each around the three bigger Great Lakes, and then one for the two lower ones, just last year. I also survived the Great Lakes Challenge, along with two other guys on Harleys, in which we circumnavigated all five of those same lakes, some 2,750 miles, on a four-day ride. That was fun!

More recently I've focused on even longer rides! Although I've been concentrating on biking [fewer] miles per day, so there is now time for some Billy and Wyatt–style "flower sniffing" along the way.

Now that I'm retired, I plan to do a lot more of that kind of riding. I would now like to go full circle and do an Easy Rider *route someday.*[204]

Jim Griffin always wanted to take that *Easy Rider* route himself:

First, let me set the stage. I was born on May 15, 1947, in Dallas, Texas, to a beer-drinking rodeo cowboy and a mother who was orphaned at birth. I never knew a grandparent. I was always moving from one school to the next, always the outsider. I never built those close friendships as a kid.

My first ride on a motorcycle was when I was about ten years old. My cousin had a Harley-Davidson; I guess it was a 1930s model. It was a moment in time which I have never forgotten.

Fast-forward: My first bike was a Honda 250 Scrambler. A series of bikes followed. Unlike when I was an outsider kid, I began to make friends with mutual interests—bikers.

Now to the real subject: Easy Rider. *My first introduction to the movie was in 1969, as [it was] for most of us. I came away from the theater with a new appreciation about riding with friends. The main characters in the movie were like my childhood heroes, the cowboy and his sidekick. From that day on I knew that someday I would follow the route from LA to New Orleans.*

There was a dirt-bike phase in there, too. I liked dirt-biking because you could get out in the sticks, build a campfire, and see the stars, Easy Rider–style. *In 1972 I got my first Harley-Davidson, and I felt I had arrived.*

[The year] 1973 brought me a new profession. I was now a barber, with an Easy Rider *poster on the wall of [my] shop. It was inside*

work, no heavy lifting, although it meant that I would be working a lot, and without much time off to complete my longtime dream of following that Easy Rider *route.*

I did a lot of riding, anyway: Colorado, Sturgis, Daytona, and the ROT (Republic of Texas, naturally) Biker Rally. But I could only be out of town for a few days at a time—not enough to get all the way to New Orleans, that's for sure.

Enter Barbara. We had been dating on and off, and married in 1999. I did a lot more riding, right up until I retired in 2010. Then I realized that there were no more excuses. I now had time to complete a trip I'd been wanting to do since the night I saw Easy Rider *in 1969, forty-plus years earlier. And Barbara encouraged me!*

I finally did it! Route 66 from LA, through Death Valley to Ballarat, standing on a corner in Winslow, Arizona; Flagstaff, Monument Valley, Sunset Crater; north to Wupaki and Sacred Mountain; Amarillo; Morganza, of course; then on to New Orleans. While there I went to [St. Louis] Cemetery No. 1 (that's what it's called) in the French Quarter. Outside of town I also stopped at the spot where the movie's double murders happened along the road, to pay my respects.

Route completed after all those years, all those roads, we headed back home—with a detour to Key West first.

Yes, you could say that the movie had a lasting impression on me.[205]

Skip Wiatrolik, a lifelong easy rider, has said that he didn't see the film right when it first came out; he was a little young. But, he recalls,

my sister, her old man at the time was in a motorcycle club in the 1960s and early '70s. So, every time it came on TV, I just had to see it. For the time, that movie had everything I wanted in the world. It had it all. It had drugs, it had sex, it had rock 'n' roll, it had bikes. It had everything that was alluring for us in the 1960s and '70s. Because of Easy Rider, *I've been riding for over forty years. Because of* Easy Rider, *I decided what I wanted in my life: riding. Like, that feeling of freedom, man. That open road.*

A few years ago, I remember I was on that road, and I saw a couple bikes coming up from behind that looked just like the bikes from Easy Rider. *What a trip! So, I pulled up alongside them and looked over, maybe expecting to see someone like Hopper and Fonda, you know, and the guys on those bikes were just kids, in their twenties! And when I passed them, what am I thinking? I'm thinking that they looked fucking uncomfortable! Me, I'm in for comfort now; I've got a heated seat, stereo in my helmet; I like to hear my music.*

See, life, it changes you. You start getting mortgages, and a credit-card bill, and all of these things that you have to work for when you have two motorcycles in the garage and a '69 Camaro and a truck and a van and six dogs and three cats and an old lady. You're working quite a bit. But sometimes you have to get away, back to what matters, to that road. My wife, she gets it. I'll tell her, "I'm about ready to kill somebody!" She's like, "See ya—go!"[206]

Wiatrolik also has a more-direct connection to one of the movie's creators.

I'm a plumber. I used to work for Dennis Hopper down in his house in Venice. He always had, like, the coolest memorabilia around the house. That buckskin jacket that he wore in the movie, it was there. And the pictures he had of him and Peter Fonda when they were filming! He was just the coolest dude—laid-back, [just] the most welcoming, genuine guy. I've worked for a lot of celebrities. Most of them are very, very into themselves. Not him. That's why it was such a pleasure to work for him. He was just down-to-earth, man.

Sometimes now, I'll be down in Venice, and I'll drive by his old house, and I'll remember that. You know, I wanted back then to ask him about the movie, but I never did. I wish I would have. I wish I would have said something to him then, about how important Easy Rider *was to me. About how he was one of us.*

I bet he would have liked that.[207]

Jim Leonard is a motorcycle builder and the world's greatest *Easy Rider* collector. He owns mementos from the film which even Dennis Hopper would have envied. Leonard's collection includes items as large as a Captain America bike replica, and as small as a beer can from Melancon's Café (the brand is "Jax"), as well as props, photography, costumes, ephemera, and memorabilia. Leonard's feelings on the film itself and its influence on his life were recorded for the documentary *On the Trail of* Easy Rider: *40 Years On . . . Still Searching for America:*

> *My dad, and I, he wasn't the kind of guy that, you know, you went and did father and son things with, you know—the fishing, the football. The thing that galvanized our relationship was motorcycles. To me, when I see the motorcycles, I ride the motorcycles, I remember my dad. I remember him teaching me. I remember him telling me, you know, if I thought I was too good, too smart, that the thing would come back to bite me. I still do ridiculous things, like, I'll just turn the throttle upside down and hang on, even at my age! I don't know, you get lost in your own thoughts; it gives you time to think about the past, the present. You're all alone out there. I mean, even if someone's around you, you're still trapped with your own thoughts. There's nothing like heading out on the open road that just gives you that rebellious feeling. You're out there, you're free to do. It's unbelievable. To me, it's America.*[208]

In many ways, George Christie epitomizes the outlaw life, and the rewards, and consequences, and damnations anyone who is brave enough to follow that road can expect. Christie has said that "some people run away and join the circus. I ran away and joined the Hells Angels." A former president of the Los Angeles charter and the founder of the Ventura branch of the club, his advocacy of uniting all biker clubs against the police, whom he considered to be their common enemy, made him a target of persecution within the establishment, and eventually, among his fellow members. He resigned his presidency of the Ventura charter, and the Hells Angels in 2011, after forty years as a member, leader, and spokesperson in that organization, because he felt like they had become the people they had once rebelled against. Having survived numerous jail sentences, indictments, and botched judicial procedures, today he works as a consultant for defense attorneys and offenders.

Christie's relationship with *Easy Rider* is socially conscious, political, and wistfully introspective.

As the sixties came to a close, I had both feet firmly planted in the Outlaw Bike Culture. Over that decade I had watched the world change before my eyes. On December 6, 1969, for many, new hopes and dreams slowly slipped away at the Altamont Free Concert. It was held fifty miles east of San Francisco and it brought the sixties to a violent end. Personally, I think it started long before Meredith Hunter was stabbed to death as he pointed a gun at the stage the Rolling Stones performed on. For me it was a series of events that began with the public execution of JFK, the introduction of widespread drug use in white Middle America, and the public's questioning of our leaders. We had the intelligence to put a man on the moon, but not to keep us out of a war we couldn't win. America elected Richard Nixon as president to lead us out of harm's way, only later to resign in disgrace as he faced impeachment. Everything seemed out of order; even the lifestyle I had chosen was now a caricature of itself, with a flood of B-biker movies. So, when Easy Rider *came out, I wasn't sure what to expect. But as I walked out of that theater, I knew they had got it right. Whether on a conscious or subconscious level, they had encapsulated it all in ninety-five minutes of film.*

If you don't agree, that's okay. Because here we are, fifty years later, still having a conversation about Easy Rider.[209]

Like everyone else involved, Alan Dunn, a contributor to this volume, also seems to have his own *Easy Rider* story. Get out of his way . . .

Easy Rider. *It's a fifty-year-old movie now. Has it had an influence on me? Yeah, I'd have to say that it has.*

I first saw Easy Rider *when I was twenty-one years old, almost twenty years after it was released in theaters. I was living in Long*

Beach, California, at the time, and a friend of mine suggested we watch it. We both loved motorcycles, so we went out and rented the movie.

I distinctly remember when the opening credits ran; hearing "Born to Be Wild," and watching Peter Fonda and Dennis Hopper make miles across the country—"Looking for adventure, and whatever comes our way . . ." It ignited a spark in my twenty-one-year-old brain, and I wanted to do the same thing. Riding across America— that sure did seem like something that I wanted to do.

Looking back, I think that moment influenced the course of my life.

I sat there for the rest of the movie and just ate it all up. The camping scenes, the open road. The, well, the freedom. I still remember that when the movie ended, both of us were in a bit of a shock. We sat there silently for a few minutes while we tried to process what had just happened.

Life is funny; as I look back, there are a few times, very few, where you just know, even at the moment when it happens, that things have just shifted into an entirely different tangent for you. These are the times where it becomes obvious, maybe years later, that if you hadn't been influenced, right then, and at that crossroads, at that time, that your life might have veered off into an entirely different direction. I'm talking about things like getting married, or having a child, of course, or about the influence on a person's life of a mentor, or a parent. Some of these impacts are big, some are small, but they all still have an effect—again, big or small, on the course we steer.

Easy Rider, for me, is right in there as one of those.

I bought my first street bike in LA the very next day. See what I mean? I couldn't afford a Harley, so I bought a 1982 Honda that at least looked like one. I paid 750 bucks, cash, and I loved that bike. It was a vehicle for freedom to me. And somehow, I now knew that I very much needed that freedom.

A key to finding that freedom, for me, seemed to involve getting out of California. So, I loaded everything that mattered onto my bike and headed back to Utah. I had a Sony Walkman at the time, and I have a really distinct memory of listening to "A Horse with No Name" as I crossed through the 110-degree heat of the Mojave Desert. I also have a distinct memory of the rightness of the open road, and of riding on that road. I knew that this feeling was something that I needed to have in my life. I loved it. I loved every single thing about it.

What happened next? I came home, I met the love of my life, I got married. And I kept riding.

I rode the hell out of that bike. The goal was always to find a new road, a new town to ride, a place to drink it in, to learn a thing. There's a Zen to riding that I love the hell out of.

I've always thought that you need at least three days for a killer riding experience; the first day, to drain out all the bullshit; the second day, to start feeling like yourself; and the third day is pure inspiration. Life, love, the good and the bad, it all comes into perspective. Yeah . . . Zen.

There isn't anything else like it that I've found.

My bike eventually gave up the ghost. But I just went out to a bike boneyard, found a new engine for it, put it in, and I kept on riding!

I rode for a couple more years, until that bike finally died again, this time for good. I'll never forget pushing it off the back of my truck and into the local landfill. And I gotta admit it, I wept. I had put in miles and . . . years of experiences on that bike . . .

I didn't know at the time if, or when, I'd get another one, either.

But I got lucky. My business had done well, and eventually I discovered that I could finally afford a Harley. I looked at one that was the same color as my original bike, and kinda fell in love with it. So, I bought that Harley, and, again, I kept riding.

Years later, I was coming home on that bike from a Route 66 ride, heading south out of Flagstaff Arizona. My ass hurt, and I stopped to take a break. On long rides, your butt feels like it's sitting on a cinderblock. But a good fifteen-minute break will reset you, and you can power it out for the next hundred miles till you have to stop again to get gas.

So, I pulled over in front of what looked like an old home, just out of town. And as I climbed down, I, well, although I'd never been there before, I recognized the place. It was the sacred Mountain Gas

Station, from Easy Rider, *where Peter Fonda and Dennis Hopper, and that hippie, had stopped and gotten gas.*

I was curious, and so I knocked on the door. The owner came out, and confirmed that this was indeed the spot from Easy Rider, *and he told me that another location for the same movie was just ten miles up the road.*

Reenergized, I followed that road, and yes, I recognized the buttes and hills from the background for those riding scenes where, remember it? The Band had played "The Weight" on the soundtrack—one of my favorite parts in the movie.

So, I started thinking about other locations from the movie. Some of those locations, like what I'd just seen, were places I'd already ridden and just recognized; most of them, I had no clue where they were.

Over the next few years, and many rides, following the trail of Easy Rider *became the inspiration, the excuse, really, for some really good rides. What the hell—the best part of riding is having a loose location or an idea to aim for, and figuring out the rest along the way. So, using* Easy Rider *as an inspiration, I zigzagged between Los Angeles and Louisiana, asking questions and trying to imagine how the decades since the movie came out might have changed the landscape. Usually, I'd find what I was looking for, too, at least eventually.*

So, one night, I'd had a couple of beers, and I then wrote a blog post about it. I forgot all about this post until a couple of days later, when, bored, I checked to see how well it was doing.

My post had gone viral. I was getting ten thousand–plus hits a day!

In the motorcycle world, turns out, other riders out there had wanted to see the same thing as me. They wanted to relive, and to revisit, Easy Rider.

This did not escape the attention of EagleRider Tours, the largest motorcycle touring company in the world. One day I got a call from them. Seems they wanted to start an official Easy Rider *tour, and they wanted me to be a part of that.*

I was very proud to contribute, establishing the routes for the tour and going along on that tour, telling stories, and sharing stories about

Easy Rider *with other fans over the course of two exciting weeks on the road.*

On every tour, I got to meet riders from all over the world, including the US, the UK, Germany, Brazil, Australia, Spain, and Belgium. It was a privilege to ride with some of these guys, Easy Rider *fans from around the world, all. There is something very special that happens when you ride with someone for two weeks. Our adventures took us from the highways of California to the brutal heat of Death Valley, from the vistas of Monument Valley to the beauty and art of New Mexico, and finally we concluded amid the history and culture of New Orleans. Riding with total strangers at the start of a trip eventually creates a bond of camaraderie and friendship that I've not seen anywhere else. All thanks to* Easy Rider.

Easy Rider. *It's a fifty-year-old movie now. It's pretty dated, and you hardly ever see it on TV. You can find it in the DVD bargain bin of your local Walmart sometimes. But it's still around. In fact, part of what keeps people like me coming back to it after all those years, and yes, all those miles, actually has very little to do with the movie itself. I don't even see the storyline when I watch it now. Now I just flash back to the memories of my own rides, and the people I met on those rides.*

It also seems that there are two kinds of people who keep returning to Easy Rider: *There are those who like it for the social commentary, sure; and [then] there are those who like it for the riding.*

This might surprise you, after my remarks above, but I like the social commentary. It's a snapshot of the times. As I see it, in Easy Rider, *you had these three people who were trying to be free, and hey, just trying to get to Mardi Gras, too. But one of them gets killed, and so, according to Wyatt at the end of the movie, "they blew it." I think that statement—who cares what it means—is one reason why the movie has stuck around. People like mulling over that message, for whatever reason.*

I think the other reason the movie was—is—popular, even among those who have never thought of straddling a bike, is that there are three distinct characters, one (or maybe two) for anyone, for everyone, in the audience to relate to. Billy is the wild man, and certain people, certain types of people, gravitate toward that. Dennis

Hopper certainly was a wild man. Wyatt is his opposite, the thoughtful person, more prone to spending time worrying and figuring things out. He's the one looking for America. He's the one that can't find it. It's hard to imagine Billy worrying about "finding America," right? George Hanson, the third part of the triangle, is just cool; he's smart and funny. He's the guy, who, like me, found America by getting onto a bike. The three of them, different as they are, they're friends, and the whole contrast works.

Do you have time for a couple of observations here? Good.

Take the café scene, which is a pivotal part of the movie. The three of them roll into Morganza, Louisiana, and are refused service, simply because they are different. The long hair, the bikes . . . All that shit. The supposition of the movie is that the townspeople kill George Hanson because he is different. The message is that hate, hate killed George Hanson. Later on, hate Kills Billy and Wyatt too.

The good news is that, as a whole, I don't believe we're like that anymore.

I think I'm qualified to say this because I've traveled the country; I went searching for America. I think I've found it.

And it's not a bad place.

You see, I know the people of Morganza, for example, and I've found them to be a good and genuine people. Not racist, not afraid of change, and certainly not hateful. I mean, I'm a shaved-headed biker, tattoos up and down both arms, I ride a Harley. And yet, in contrast to the violence portrayed in the movie, the people of Morganza, well, they've treated me with nothing but respect. I count many of those people as friends.

So, I think the world has changed since 1969.

Also, did you know that when they were scouting locations for the movie, and that later, when they were shooting the movie, the Easy Rider *crew avoided Texas? There were stories about hippies venturing into Texas and having their hair (and other things) shaved off with rusty razor blades!*

But, flash-forward fifty years: Peter Fonda, a little while ago, tweeted about ripping Barron Trump, the president's youngest child, from his mother's arms and throwing him to pedophiles! After the backlash, he apologized. Was Fonda's own, fifty-year-old Easy Rider *message about acceptance lost on him?*

In fifty years, maybe we've just changed the focus of our hate. Some of the messages of Easy Rider *have just been flipped. That's where the world stands, at least in my eyes.*

The whole point of Easy Rider *was, as they put it then, how you could go looking for America and not find it anywhere. Less hate, more respect.*

I guess we still have a way to go.

Yeah, Easy Rider *has influenced me. So now, here's my question to you: Has the movie influenced you? Has the movie really made an impact? Have we gotten better, since 1969?*

Some of the bikers we talked to above, as we have learned, struck out to follow in the tire treads, often literally, of Wyatt and Billy. But the cult of *Easy Rider* is not made up of just fans and gangs and groupies and hippies and yuppies. Journalists and sociologists and filmmakers and even organized tours have themselves set out, either literally or intellectually, in search of America, in search of *Easy Rider*, and in search of whatever *Easy Rider* might mean.

The first notice in the mainstream press of the cult of *Easy Rider* came in 1989 with a satirical piece in *Premiere* magazine, called "*Easy Rider* Revisited." The two young writers, Jack Barth and Trey Ellis, set off to follow the trail of Wyatt and Billy, although, *Lost in America*–style, Barth and Ellis did it using four wheels instead of two, because they said they couldn't find anyone in the vicinity of the Los Angeles International Airport to rent them choppers.

Peter Fonda, they reckoned, would be too busy as "the Olivier of the cable-ready action flick"[210] to participate, but they did stop by Dennis Hopper's house ("He wasn't home"[211]) and saw Jack Nicholson's gate ("He didn't come out"[212]) before hitting the open road. They then meandered on to Las Vegas, Monument Valley, and Taos, New Mexico.

In Taos, Barth and Ellis visited the city jail, albeit not the one in the movie, which they acknowledged was then an art gallery. But while there, they did chat up a local cop, who admitted that "I know Dennis Hopper; I arrested him once. We all did."[213]

In Morganza, Louisiana, the duo discovered that Melancon's Café was closed and boarded up, but they arranged to meet up with three actual *Easy Rider* cast members at another, nearby diner: Hayward Robillard, who is billed in the film as "Cat Man" (the one with the famous Caterpillar-brand yellow hat), Paul Guedry Jr. (who played "Customer #4"), and Rose LeBlanc (who was "Girl #3"). *Easy Rider*, incidentally, would turn out to be the only film credit achieved by any of them—both because Screen Actors Guild rules allow non-actors to only make one film appearance each in SAG signatory films, and also because *Easy Rider* had been the only time, thus far, that any of the trio had been asked to perform on camera.

Robillard still seemed to be slightly upset, even after twenty years, that Dennis Hopper had apparently reneged on a promise he had made to send him Billy's buckskin jacket after the movie wrapped. "That lying bastard never did," he recalled sadly. Too bad, because, "it would have been great for deer hunting."[214]

LeBlanc, who was thirty-seven in 1989, would have been only seventeen in 1969, but she said that the crew had invited her to an after-shoot "pot party," regardless. She demurred, and told them that "my parents have enough Tupperware."[215]

Barth and Ellis eventually swung through New Orleans, couldn't find Madam Tinkertoy's House of Blue Lights, and so drove on to Orlando, where, as befitting two 1980s rebels, the duo ended their *Easy Rider* odyssey at Disney World.

For those unwilling to head out on the highway by themselves, it is still possible to experience what Billy and Captain America did; the good parts, anyway. As Alan Dunn mentioned above, EagleRider Tours, which, like Billy and Captain America, is based out of Los Angeles, offers participants a chance to follow in their heroes' boot steps for a fifteen-day "*Easy Rider* Movie Tour" odyssey across America. Like in the movie, the tourists ride motorcycles from Los Angeles into Death Valley, across the Mojave Desert, through Needles, California, on to Flagstaff, Arizona, through Monument Valley and Durango, Colorado, and into

Dennis Hopper's beloved Taos, New Mexico. Unlike the film crew, which avoided Texas because of its policy about "long-hairs," the tour then boldly crosses through Abilene and Austin on the way to Louisiana. Again, unlike in the movie, this journey concludes in New Orleans, with no violence by the locals anticipated. EagleRider also boasts on their website of having a replica Captain America bike available to the guests for photo shoots and excursions.

Not everyone who had their lives changed by *Easy Rider* took their obsession out on the road. Sometimes they took that obsession home with them. And sometimes this fixation with the *Easy Rider* lifestyle affected the family of those who were fixated.

Illeana Douglas, a very popular and respected actress, surprised her fans in 2015 when she published *I Blame Dennis Hopper*, a memoir which amusingly describes what happened when her parents saw *Easy Rider* and her father became convinced that when Billy said "That's what it's all about, man!" he was telling *him* to change his life. Which he did.

Douglas's father quit his lucrative nine-to-five job and started a commune. Still not satisfied, he grew a mustache like Dennis Hopper's, raised goats, wrote poetry, and even adopted his own hippie named Tom. Tom also had a mustache, wore a fringed leather jacket, drove a chopper, and ended every sentence with "man." "To his credit, Tom the Hippie was an excellent hippie," she concedes.[216]

Eventually her father did hit that road, presumably to find America, leaving his family behind. Illeana later got to work with Peter Fonda in *Grace of My Heart* (1996)—in a scene set in a commune. "When I looked at the rushes of my smoking a joint with Peter Fonda, I thought, yup, my real life and my movie life have come full circle."[217] She also costarred in *Search and Destroy* (1995), with, yup, Dennis Hopper. "I told him this story, basically blaming him for everything that had happened to me, and he grinned sheepishly and said 'Sorry.'"[218]

Perhaps because of her personal experiences, Illeana Douglas also has a unique take on *Easy Rider*'s place in the world, and how that world has changed since the movie was released. "*Easy Rider* represents a time when *freedom* meant freedom from material things, freedom from driving in six lanes of traffic to work twelve hours a day at a job you hate," she has said. "Freedom in 1969 was the land—the land of the free and the brave. Freedom was peace and love. The word *freedom* has been co-opted; today, it means the freedom to be selfish, to carry guns. Freedom to hurt the land and its inhabitants for the sake of commerce. *Easy Rider* reminds us how far we have strayed from that journey."[219]

In addition to being blamed for breaking up families, *Easy Rider* has taken some heat for denigrating the Deep South. Surely no motorcyclist since 1969 has been able to cruise past a pickup truck with a gun rack, or stop at a small-town diner south of the Mason-Dixon, without thinking about the movie, and not in a happy way. Peter Fonda has always found these accusations that the film is critical of the South baseless. "We could have gone through Detroit or Buffalo and been ripped up just as easily by a bunch of geeks up there," he has said.[220]

Hopper also was uncharacteristically careful not to offend Southerners in interviews after the film came out. Although he did say in 1969 that "I know that if I'd come in there actually traveling across the country, or if me or Peter and Jack Nicholson had walked into that restaurant without a movie company behind us, and those men had been sitting in there, we'd have been in a lot of trouble."[221]

Easy Rider has even been accused of bearing some responsibility for the cocaine epidemic in the 1970s. This accusation has been leveled at the film by a surprising accuser, too: Dennis Hopper. Hopper told writer Peter Biskind in 1998 that "the cocaine problem in the United States is really because of me. There was no cocaine [on the street] before *Easy Rider*. After *Easy Rider* it was everywhere."[222]

CHAPTER SIX

End of the Ride

EASY RIDER PROFOUNDLY AFFECTED MANY OF THOSE WHO EXPERIENCED it in 1969, and has continued to do so in the decades that have followed. As has been noted, the film also continues to haunt the ever-dwindling surviving members of the cast and crew.

"I can't believe it's been fifty years since *Easy Rider*," Henry Jaglom said when I ruined his day by informing him of this fact. "I just—I can't, I can't really believe it . . ."[223] Jaglom, of course, went on to a very long and idiosyncratic career as a filmmaker and raconteur, a career somewhat inspired by that of his good friend, Orson Welles. Among his achievements as a director was *Tracks* (1976), one of the first American films to deal with the conflict in Vietnam, and which also featured one of Dennis Hopper's best performances.

Donn Cambern, the credited editor on the film, scored an Oscar nomination for *Romancing the Stone* (1984). His other credits include *The Last Picture Show* (1971), *Time After Time* (1979), and *The Bodyguard* (1992). In 2002 he became a governor of the Academy of Motion Picture Arts and Sciences. "I was self-taught," he has said. "But I've been around editors a lot, and they were always talking about the rules, which I thought was nonsense. But I finally decided that, as an editor, I do have two rules. Don't bore, and don't confuse."[224]

Bert Schneider, who hired Cambern and Jaglom, and gave a lot of other creative people a foothold in the business, went on to become one of the architects of New Hollywood. His ability to work with the studios for money and for distribution, while remaining largely autonomous, is the business model for many independently produced features even today. Screenwriter Jacob Brackman said of Schneider: "People thought he really had taste and integrity and energy and was making up very creative kinds of deals. His reputation was basically, he'll take care of you. All these people got little pieces of *Easy Rider*, down to the secretaries. It was almost unheard of. People really looked up to him. He could just do what he wanted."[225]

Henry Jaglom seconds that. "Bert was the single most significant person, post-1950s, in terms of producers, of what [David O.] Selznick had been before . . . He trusted filmmakers and gave them complete freedom."[226] "He was just the guy," Cambern agrees.[227] "He was so cool, it was, like, frightening," actor Richard Dreyfuss adds.[228] "Bert knew and loved film, but he knew and loved filmmakers even more," Peter Davis, the director of Schneider's documentary *Hearts and Minds* (1974), has said.[229]

The problem was that Schneider wanted to make films, but without a studio to absorb those film's occasional losses—which, as the years piled up, became less occasional—he found that he was gambling his company and his future every time he rolled the dice. He won an Oscar for *Hearts and Minds*, and gave a controversial acceptance speech which seemed to be praising North Vietnam, which was perhaps why he failed to get a film distributed for three years after that. "Everybody wanted to be Bert Schneider, and then nobody wanted to be Bert Schneider," Dreyfuss has said.[230]

Eventually, as usually happens with small production companies, BBS was absorbed by a big production company—ironically, Columbia Pictures. Schneider largely retired after that. Sadly, unheralded as one of the first independent Hollywood producers, Bert Schneider died in 2011.

"I always thought Bert Schneider was kind of mean. He was scary," Karen Black has said. "I met Bob [Rafelson, Schneider's partner] later; he was the beautiful rebel kind of guy."[231]

Rafelson used *Head* as a springboard to a successful directing career. "Of course, *Head* is an utterly and totally fragmented film," he remembered. "Among other reasons for making it was that I thought I would never get to make another movie, so I might as well make fifty to start out with and put them all in the same feature."[232] *Five Easy Pieces* (1970), with Jack Nicholson, followed *Head*, which would be the second of six collaborations between the star and director. Rafelson's career as a director would continue through 2002's *No Good Deed*. Today he is retired and lives in Colorado.

The third Raybert/BBC partner, Steven Blauner, worked in distribution and as an occasional producer until 1987. In the movie *Beyond the Sea* (2004), on which he was a consultant, he was played by John Goodman. Blauner died in 2015.

William "Bill" Hayward, the coproducer whom Fonda and Hopper brought to the project, had family connections to both men, as has been noted. Consequently, he was much criticized at Raybert and at Columbia for being both a family friend and a family member. The truth is, he was probably the only person who could have kept the project on track during Hopper's delirious excesses *because* of his insider status, and so he deserves more respect than he ever received for getting the project finished under extremely difficult personal conditions.

Difficult personal conditions ran in the family for Hayward. That family's problems were chronicled in his sister Brooke's 1977 memoir *Haywire*, which Bill Hayward produced as a TV miniseries in 1980. Hayward continued to work with Fonda, and Fonda's Pando Productions, on *The Hired Hand* (1971), *Idaho Transfer* (1973), and *Wanda Nevada* (1979), all of which Fonda directed, as well as on some of Fonda's acting projects. "[Hayward] was kind of a wild rich boy, and then one day he just decided to become a lawyer. So, he did. He just did it! He became an extremely good lawyer," David McGiffert, a friend who worked with him often, has marveled.[233]

Hayward also shared with Peter Fonda a love of motorcycles. He was a proud member of The Uglies motorcycle club, and later brought Fonda in as a member as well. He was nearly killed in a 2003 motorcycle accident, the persistent injuries from which probably led to his death from a self-inflicted gunshot wound in the trailer (purchased for him by his friend, actor Larry Hagman) he was living in, in 2008. Dennis Hopper, when reached for comment after the tragedy, perfunctorily relayed that Hayward "was a wonderful man, and this is a great tragedy for our family."[234]

David McGiffert was more articulate, saying, "I admired Bill in ways I do not admire many people. He was an unusual being. As inscrutable as he was, there was a vulnerability and an intelligence that I have rarely seen matched in anyone."[235] McGiffert attended Bill Hayward's funeral, held in Ojai at Larry Hagman's house:

I say house, but it was like something out of The Arabian Nights. *A spectacular, unbelievable place, many levels, with open courtyards and gardens—it was just ridiculous. The mix there was really bizarre. Larry just opened his house to all these Hollywood people, and bikers and fringe people, because Bill kind of operated on the fringes of everything, and knew a lot of people from a lot of walks of life. And they all loved him and revered him and wanted to be there to celebrate his life. The finale was that they had a cannon, a small cannon below Larry's house on a little bluff. The bikers went down there and they were playing music. These bikers loaded Bill's ashes into the cannon, and at a certain point during these proceedings, [they] blasted his ashes over the countryside with a resounding cannon-type roar! That's a way to go that he would have approved of.*[236]

Most of the legendary customizers who built, or influenced, or carried on the traditions of the bikes in *Easy Rider* are gone. Benny Hardy died in 1994; Cliff "Soney" Vaughs, in 2016; and Larry Marcus, in 2017. Denver Mullins was killed in a tragic drag-boat accident in 1992, but his partner, Mondo, "the Godfather of Choppers" to his peers, has now relocated to Reno, Nevada, and carries on the so-called "Swedish" tradition. When asked if he himself ever feels the need to mount one of his own masterpieces and strike out on his own long-distance ride, Mondo smiles. "Yeah, there's nothing like sticking a broken half of a toothbrush in your back pocket and following the sun."[237]

Sugar Bear, as well, another one of the last of a breed, is still chopping bikes in his shop in Springville, California, as he has been since 1971. His motto is, "If it ain't long, it's wrong."

Although most of the men who made the bikes have ridden into the dark, there have been persistent rumors, and sometimes more than rumors, that an original Captain America bike may have survived. Obviously, this holy grail of motorcycles, easily the most famous cycle in the world, would be a priceless collectable to anyone lucky enough to attain it.

In 2014, chopper aficionados, film buffs, and former hippies were all stunned when the Profiles in History auction house in California announced that they were in possession of a screen-used Captain America bike. The owner, Michael Eisenberg, claimed that, yes, the bikes had been stolen from Tex Hall's garage, and yes, had probably been broken down for parts and scattered across the country. But he also claimed that the Captain America motorcycle which had been destroyed on camera had been salvaged and rebuilt, by none other than Dan Haggerty, the future *Grizzly Adams* star, who, in addition to doing extra duty as a commune dweller in the film, had also assisted Hall as a motorcycle wrangler throughout the shoot. Haggerty claimed he was told by Dennis Hopper on location in Louisiana to just keep the remnants from that fiery climax, which Haggerty did, taking those remnants home and then painstakingly reconstructing the bike.

But how much was left to reconstruct? Peter Fonda said in 1999 that "I think the frame was bent pretty badly, and the fork was torn off. The transmission melted down into a chunk of molten aluminum. I had it here on my desk for years. The engine and gas tank were gone [destroyed], but I think the back end and seat were OK."[238]

Haggerty claimed that he Frankensteined together, piece by piece, over several years, this priceless Captain America bike, and then rode it often, an experience he likened to "going out with Marilyn Monroe."[239] Haggerty eventually sold the machine to a friend at the National Motorcycle Museum in Anamosa, Iowa, which is where Eisenberg had been lucky enough to purchase it from.

For the auction, Haggerty issued a statement that "the bike owned by Michael Eisenberg is the only authentic Captain America bike that was rebuilt from the original frame up"—which, coming from the man who did that rebuilding, makes for a convincing-enough chain of provenance. So, on the strength of this seemingly rock-solid authentication, that cycle was sold on the auction block for $1,350,000, almost $200,000 above what Profiles in History had anticipated the bike would go for.

The problem is, it seems that there is at least one more Captain America motorcycle out there—which Haggerty had also authenticated. Apparently, it seems that in 1993, Dan Haggerty had sold a Captain America bike to one Gordon Granger, who has since maintained that *this* bike was the authentic one (although a Chicago motorcycle exhibit he had loaned it to in 1999 had displayed it as a replica, which makes one wonder why Granger, if he was convinced he had the original, would have presented it this way).

In 2002, Granger asked Haggerty to give him something in writing authenticating his motorcycle, which he received. Haggerty later said that he thought he was signing something that stated Granger's was a replica. Granger was able to produce this document after the 2014 auction and thus stop that million-dollar Profiles in History sale from actually being completed.

It seems, as illustrated above, that Dan Haggerty was a less-than-reliable witness. In 1984, six years after his *Grizzly Adams* heyday, he was arrested for selling cocaine to two undercover policemen. It also eventually came out that in 2008, he had sold *yet another* Captain America cycle to the Guggenheim Museum in New York!

Even Gordon Granger, who might have benefited from convincing people of Haggerty's honesty, called the actor "one of the biggest fucking liars in the world."[240]

Eisenberg then pulled Peter Fonda into the melee, who, along with Hopper, he had occasionally had business dealings with, by claiming that the star had agreed to authenticate *his* bike, which early newspaper reports had said he was prepared to do. Eisenberg later claimed that the star had backed out because he wanted to be paid for his endorsement.

Fonda, over the years, has also been associated with a manufacturer who, in 1999, started creating purpose-built Captain America replicas, each of which Fonda agreed to authorize, and to autograph, for $24,995! But no one, it should be noted—not Fonda, not the manufacturer, and not the buyers—have ever attempted to palm these replicas off as having been used in the movie. At least, not yet.

There were also at least two duplicate Captain Americas built for publicity. "Not many people know this, but Columbia [Pictures] built two replicas for publicity purposes when the movie came out," Fonda has said. "Except they didn't run. Their engines didn't work."[241] Whatever happened to *these* Captain Americas is yet another mystery, although Granger's bike, intriguingly, has been reported not to work. So, one has to wonder: Could his be one of these replicas?

Paul d'Orléans, author of *The Chopper: The Real Story*, deserves the final word on this convoluted subject. He put it in perspective very well in 2015, stating that "while Eisenberg has the 'most legitimate' claim, it's all relative. What are you buying? Best-case scenario, you're buying the stunt bike's blown-up frame. They can claim to have pieces of the true cross, but Jesus is gone, man; he has left the building. And so has Captain America."[242]

Dan Haggerty—who may or may not have known in his heart which of the Captain America bikes was the real McCoy—echoing the fate of Bill Hayward, never fully recovered from a 1991 motorcycle crash which left the burly actor temporarily in a coma. The former *Grizzly Adams* star died in 2017.

The whereabouts of the other *Easy Rider* cycle wranglers, the machine-gun-wielding Tex Hall and his assistant, Gypsy, or even, come to think of it, what their real names were, is currently unknown.

As the Captain America bikes have appeared and disappeared and been verified and discredited over the years, biker culture and an appreciation of the biker lifestyle has waxed and waned as well in the decades since *Easy Rider*. In 2009, Gary Lawson of *Rolling Stone* magazine scoffed at the Harley-Davidson image, saying that "98 percent of it is dentists who were in college when *Easy Rider* came out. That's why the brand Harley-Davidson is dying. You ever watch Harley-Davidson guys riding around now? They're all the same age as Peter Fonda and Dennis Hopper!"[243]

Recently, the TV series *Sons of Anarchy* (2008–2014) has restored some of the outlaw glamour to the biker lifestyle, but many bikers feel there has been a persistent erosion of interest in that lifestyle, due to the rise of hip-hop, which has supplemented motorcycle clubs as a potential outlaw lifestyle choice for many young people.

Of course, in every culture in the world, that culture's pirates or Vikings or Huns were eventually replaced by people who came later and emulated their predecessors' hedonistic lifestyles by taking pieces of those lifestyles and adapting it all into something more "acceptable." And yet, in every community, a few cowboys and mountain men and 1-percenters continue on in their own idiosyncratic, outlaw ways, even while those outside that lifestyle romanticize it from afar, writing songs and making movies about that lifestyle, and then trying to kill those who practice it. As noted, this is one of the themes, so prevalent in Westerns, which probably attracted Peter Fonda to the material to begin with.

Hollister, California—where the so-called Hollister riot occurred, and which first drew the world's attention to the 1-percenter in 1947—now does everything it can to attract the same "dangerous" element that originally horrified the locals and the rest of the nation. Every year the city hosts a "Hollister Motorcycle Rebel Rally," with live music and drag races, and numerous events centered around two local dives, aptly named the Wild One Saloon and Johnny's Bar and Grill, both of which now proudly celebrate the biker lifestyle.

Brooke Hayward, Hopper's sharp-tongued, estranged wife during the *Easy Rider* era, never received any of Hopper's windfall from the film's success. She confided to friends that she was afraid that Hopper would come after her with a shotgun if she tried. Three times married, the best-selling *Haywire* author now lives quietly on the East Coast.

Peter Fonda and Susan Brewer divorced in 1974. She has since worked occasionally as a casting agent and costumer.

Henry Fonda, Peter's legendary father, apparently never really mellowed toward *Easy Rider*, although he did once admit that "of course, it was the beginning of a type of movie. Not only because of the low cost, but because Peter and Dennis went out with less than a script and just ad-libbed their way through it."[244] With age, however, Henry Fonda did mellow toward his son's counterculture ways and his recreational drug use. In 1979, Fonda was directing *Wanda Nevada* and talked his father into doing a cameo as an old prospector. The elder Fonda wrote a letter to his son afterward in which he said that "in my forty-one years of making motion pictures, I've never seen a director so adored by the crew. You're a very good director, son, and please remember me in your company." "[This] was incredible," Fonda remembers. "He was dying when he made that film."[245]

Before his death in 1982, Henry Fonda's last words to Peter were, "I want you to know, son, that I love you very much." "That's closure," Peter has said.[246]

Jane Fonda, Henry's daughter and Peter's older sister, eventually won two Academy Awards. Peter's daughter Bridget, whose middle name is Jane, became a film star herself in the 1990s. She is currently married to, and has a son with, composer Danny Elfman.

John Wayne, whose politics and personality symbolized everything which *Easy Rider* was seemingly opposed to, but whose on-screen persona was not so diametrically distinct from some aspects of the counterculture as one might suppose, won his only Academy Award for *True Grit*, in 1969. Dennis Hopper, of course, had costarred in both films in that same, very eventful year. Perhaps significantly, Abbie Hoffman, also in 1969, told *Time* magazine that "I like Wayne's wholeness, his style. As for his politics, well—I suppose even cavemen felt a little admiration for the dinosaurs that were trying to gobble them up."[247]

Hoffman was perhaps missing the point: that both Wayne and '60s radicals like Hoffman were already themselves dinosaurs by 1969, although cowboys like Wayne would have known this before crusaders like Hoffman. John Wayne died in 1979, only six years after the death of his mentor, director John Ford. The year of his death, Wayne was awarded a special Gold Medal by the US Congress.

Roger Ebert, whose two reviews of *Easy Rider*, in 1969 and 1994, bookended the movie's first quarter-century, in 1975 became the first film critic to win the Pulitzer Prize for film criticism. His contentious and long-lasting partnership with co-critic Gene Siskel made the two of them the most recognizable and influential film writers in history. Ebert died in 2013.

Roger Corman, the legendary independent producer whose unerring instinct for making money failed him when he let *Easy Rider* slip through his fingers, continues to craft idiosyncratic little cinematic masterpieces and monstrosities to this day. He received an honorary Academy Award in 2009. In addition to discovering, or advancing, the careers of Fonda, Nicholson, Hopper, Kovács, and Bruce Dern, among dozens of others, he has also appeared briefly as an actor in films like *The Godfather Part II*

(1974), *The Silence of the Lambs* (1991), and *Apollo 13* (1995). Usually he plays a bureaucrat who withholds important funding.

Bruce Dern, whose photo with Peter Fonda and a motorcycle inspired *Easy Rider*, has continued to be one of Hollywood's most quirky character actors. In 2014, Dern received an Oscar nomination (his second career nomination) for his role in *Nebraska*. His friend Jack Nicholson affectionately calls the actor's idiosyncrasies "Dernsies."

Rip Torn continued to be a most welcome and in-demand performer in film, on television, and on Broadway. Yet in spite of his undeniable and hard-earned success, and his multiple Oscar, Tony, and Emmy nominations, Torn never did manage to break out into mainstream stardom as Jack Nicholson did in 1969. Rip Torn died in July 2019, coinciding almost to the day with *Easy Rider*'s fiftieth anniversary.

Donnie "Hair Bear" Derbes, who still remembers the day *Easy Rider* came to Morganza, Louisiana, long managed a local roadhouse, aptly named The Bear's Den (which closed in 2017), and now works tirelessly on local restoration projects, including reopening a long-shuttered malt shop, which he promises will include a display of *Easy Rider* memorabilia.

On the other side of town, Arnold Hess Jr., who was the deputy sheriff in the diner scene, and in Morganza, said in 2009 that "I've only seen the entire movie one time. I didn't like it. I don't like it. And I hope I never see it again."[248] Hayward "Cat Man" Robillard, whose first name was actually Francis and who was the most menacing of the extras in that diner, died in 2003, presumably still waiting for Dennis Hopper to send him a buckskin jacket.

Like Melancon's Café, many of the original *Easy Rider* locations are no longer standing, or have been repurposed. As noted earlier, the old Taos, New Mexico, jailhouse has become a series of expensive art galleries (by name, it was first Bryan's Gallery, but more recently it has been renamed Tito's Gallery). The La Contenta Bar for a time was a furniture store. The Pine Breeze Inn in Bellemont, Arizona, where the NO VACANCY sign chased off Wyatt and Billy, is now abandoned, although a sun-bleached poster for *Easy Rider* still hangs in a window. The Sacred Mountain gas station outside of Wupatki, Arizona, apparently now serves as a private residence, although the owner, again apparently, isn't answering the door any longer. Even Route 66 itself, the mother road, was decertified as a highway by the federal government in 1985. Up in Toronto, the Hillcrest Motel, where Fonda first conceived his "Western-biker flick" was closed in 2009, and has since been demolished.

Even Columbia Pictures, which begrudgingly let *Easy Rider* fall into its lap—and consequently ended up with one of the biggest hits in its history—moved out of its studio in Hollywood, where Raybert was headquartered, in 1972, to cohabitate with Warner Bros. in Burbank. In 1989, Sony, the Japanese electronics giant, purchased Columbia for $3.4 billion and moved the studio to the old MGM lot in Culver City. Today, Columbia continues to be one of the world's major producers of "filmed" entertainment.

László Kovács used *Easy Rider* as a springboard to a career as one of Hollywood's most acclaimed cinematographers. Those controversial lens-flare effects utilized in *Easy Rider*, which caused some critics and even some fellow cinematographers to accuse him of incompetence in 1969, were widely imitated and adapted by other cameramen throughout the following decades. Today these same "shimmering" effects are often created in postproduction and inside a computer to add "realism" to the scene being photographed.

Kovács's many credits, some with lens flares, include *Five Easy Pieces* (1970), *Paper Moon* (1973), *Shampoo* (1975), *Ghostbusters* (1984), and *My Best Friend's Wedding* (1997).

About *Easy Rider*, Kovács once said, "I came from a very small village in Hungary. I came back to visit and my mother said, 'There is this young man who is a hairdresser in a village, and he wants to shake your hand. Please don't deny him.' I said, 'Okay, no problem.' So, this man comes over to our house, and he looks at me and says, 'Let me [shake] your hand.' He says, 'This movie changed my life. I saw it thirty-four times!' I said, 'What was it—what was it that changed?' He said, 'Everything. I see the world differently now.'"[249]

László Kovács died in 2007 in Beverly Hills.

Luke Askew, who played the unnamed hitchhiker who rides behind Captain America on the "bitch saddle" (biker parlance), was a genuine counterculture character who impressed Hopper on the *Cool Hand Luke* set by refusing to cut his hair (he wore a hat to hide his locks), although later, for *The Green Berets* (1968), he did allow his hair to be cut, probably because he was afraid to say no to John Wayne. With or without long hair, Askew remained a fixture on both the big screen and the small, almost until the moment of his death in 2012.

Karen Black would go on to become a major leading lady on film and in television in the 1970s. Her brief role in *Easy Rider* would lead to a breakout (and Oscar-nominated) performance in *Five Easy Pieces* (1970), opposite Jack Nicholson. Black's career then evolved into a rather eclectic mix of big-budget leading-lady roles, and quirkier fare. In 1975–1976 alone, for example, she could be seen doing memorable work in *Airport 1975*, *The Day of the Locust*, Robert Altman's *Nashville*, Alfred Hitchcock's *Family Plot*, the supernatural thriller *Burnt Offerings*, and the TV classic *Trilogy of Terror*. The latter, true to its name, is notorious for having terrorized a generation of viewers.

As she aged into character roles, Black continued to act regularly, even as other leading ladies of her generation were unable to do so. Her distinctive, slightly cross-eyed look made her perfect for either villainous or comedic roles. Always a raconteur, she also dabbled in playwriting, worked in independent or experimental films, and appeared in music videos. Karen Black died from cancer in 2013.

Her cohort, Toni Basil, had worked with Bruce Conner on the experimental film *BREAKAWAY* (1966). Dennis Hopper once called Conner "the most important artist of the twentieth century,"[250] so it's surprising that according to Fonda, Hopper originally objected to Basil's casting. However, having also worked as a choreographer/dancer on *Head*, Basil had the inside track, and significantly, like Black, she was also willing to work for scale.

Toni Basil would later appear with both Nicholson and Black again, in *Five Easy Pieces* (1970). She has long been reluctant to talk about her appearance in *Easy Rider*, as she reportedly felt like she was bullied by the director into disrobing for the cemetery sequence. In spite of this incident, Basil has never been one to be bullied. In 1969 she was already almost a decade into a laudable career as an actress, filmmaker, dancer, recording artist, and choreographer, a career which continues today. The millions of teenage fans of her 1981 number-one hit song "Mickey," which she performed in one of the first music videos ever, would have been astonished to learn that their cheerleading heartthrob was already thirty-eight years old at the time.

Most of the other actors whose résumés include an appearance in *Easy Rider* are no longer among us. Warren Finnerty, the old rancher, died in 1974, as did Lea Marmer, aka Madam Tinkertoy. Jack Nicholson's friend, Luana Anders, who played Lisa, passed away in 1996, Carrie Snodgress, in 2004. Phil Spector has been incarcerated since 2009. In fact, of the more-prominent hired actors, as opposed to the non-actors, who were conscripted on location, only Sabrina Scharf, Helena Kallianiotes, Robert Ball, and Robert Walker, as far as we can tell, are still with us.

Behind the camera, production manager Paul Lewis and script supervisor Joyce King are long retired, although one imagines that their memories and dreams of *Easy Rider*, good or bad, are still vivid. Among Hopper's "New Orleans crew," Seymour Cassel scored a Best Supporting Actor Oscar nomination for 1968's *Faces*, the same year he worked for Hopper. Cassel continued to work, as an actor, not as a cinematographer, it should be noted, until his death in early 2019. His much-abused comrades, Les Blank, Alan Pariser, Richard Rust, Peter Pilafian, Baird Bryant, and Barry Feinstein are no longer working, or are no longer with us.

Jack Valenti, whose 1967 diatribe in Toronto inspired the inception of *Easy Rider*, served as the president of the Motion Picture Association of America for another thirty-seven years. He died in 2007, without ever deeming it necessary to address whether it was Peter Fonda he was targeting in his "motorcycles, sex, and drugs" speech that night.

Terry Southern was unable to sustain his mid-century winning streak. *Easy Rider*, of course, was a big success—sadly, probably the one thing he is remembered for today. But Southern remained bitter about how he was ultimately cut out of the bonanza reaped by a film for which the receptionists and stenographers in the corporate offices were given profit participation points, and he either wasn't, or unwisely refused those points himself. He also felt that Fonda and Hopper, particularly Hopper, minimized his contributions to the screenplay, although even Hopper, if pressed, would usually admit that Southern did come up with the title, if nothing else, typically claiming authorship of every word that came after that title.

Southern once told *Creative Screenwriting* magazine, "You know, if Den Hopper improvises a dozen lines and six of them survive the cutting-room floor, he'll put in for screenplay credit. Now, it would be almost impossible to exaggerate his contribution to the film—but, by George, he manages to do it every time."[251]

Fonda and Hopper had to ask Southern to be credited on-screen themselves for the screenplay at all. The Writers Guild had, and has, very strict rules about producers and directors giving themselves screenplay credits. So Southern, in the spirit of camaraderie, and to his probable later regret, let them take a co-credit with him, in spite of the Guild's stated objections to him doing so.

Southern always lived and spent like the money would keep rolling in forever. And when it didn't, when quirky experimental films and quirky experimental people were no longer in vogue, he languished. In 1981 Southern was hired by his buddy, Michael O'Donoghue, as a lowly staff writer on TV's *Saturday Night Live* (1975–). At the time, the venerable late-night sketch comedy, after the temporary departure of creator Lorne Michaels, was floundering and in danger of cancellation. And Southern, insecure, overweight, alcoholic, and, by far, the oldest writer in the room, felt vulnerable and "defenseless in the snake pit of übercool wits,"[252] as his biographer has acidly described it. O'Donoghue realized that Southern's subtle and sly character comedy was a bad fit for *Saturday Night Live's* cheap laughs and bombast, especially during this particular era, considered to be one of the series' low points, but there was nothing he could do. In fact, O'Donoghue himself would be fired mid-season, with Southern following him out the door at the end of the year.

In 1994–1995 Terry Southern was hired to write PR text for Richard Branson's company, Virgin. Perry Richardson, the editor, remembers how pinpoint-precise he was with language. "I had come up with the phrase 'rabid glee' and Terry said, 'I think that's too garish.' So, we kicked around ideas for about half an hour and finally Terry said, 'I got it! How about 'grim relish!'"[253]

Terry Southern died on October 29, 1995.

"The one common link among most of [Nicholson's] roles has been the characterization of the eternal outsider, the sardonic drifter who bucks the system," is how Ephraim Katz characterizes Jack Nicholson in *The Film Encyclopedia*.[254] Nicholson has used that persona well to become one of the biggest stars in history.

Jack Nicholson's rebellious alienation perhaps unconsciously stems from his not knowing until 1974 that his "sister" June was actually his mother, and that the woman he thought was his mother was actually his grandmother. June, who had given birth at the age of seventeen, and her mother together had kept the secret from Jack until their own deaths.

Nicholson came to Hollywood in 1954 and worked as an office boy at MGM, and later, as an actor for Roger Corman and other low-budget producers. Bert Schneider liked Nicholson, but wasn't sure which side of the camera the energetic young man belonged on. That was decided by *Easy Rider*, although Nicholson has continued to write, as well as produce and occasionally direct, his own movies.

Jack Nicholson has won three Academy Awards, for *One Flew Over the Cuckoo's Nest* (1975), *Terms of Endearment* (1983), and *As Good as It Gets* (1993). For the last one, he was pitted against his fellow rider, Peter Fonda. On Oscar night, when a clip from Fonda's film, *Ulee's Gold*, was played, Dennis Hopper sat stony-faced in the audience. When it was announced that Jack had won, Hopper whooped and cheered from his seat.

Peter Fonda has often joked that when he was a struggling actor, he was known as Henry Fonda's kid; then he was Jane Fonda's kid brother; and later, he became Bridget Fonda's dad. Nonetheless, Peter Fonda has carved out a distinctive niche for himself in more than fifty years on the screen.

Alone among any other key performer on the film, Peter Fonda, as noted, actually was, and is, a motorcycle enthusiast. He was eighteen when he purchased his first motorcycle. He did it because his father asked him not to. "My father didn't want me to. It was like, in your face. As soon as I could, I bought a Harley," he told the *Los Angeles Times* in 2007.[255]

Early leading-man roles, like the vapid Dr. Cheswick in *Tammy and the Doctor* (1963), did little to challenge the actor, and did little for his career. It wasn't until *The Wild Angels* (1966) and its counterculture success that he found a role that guaranteed no one would ever confuse him with his father. Significantly, his character, for the first time on-screen, rode a motorcycle. While Fonda vehemently denies that smoking pot, riding motorcycles, and joining the counterculture was a rebellion against his old man, he has admitted that "This part saved me from playing Dean Jones roles at Disney."[256]

The Trip (1967) followed. This experience brought him together with Dennis Hopper, who costarred and directed some second-unit footage, and with Jack Nicholson, who wrote the screenplay. But *The Trip*, Fonda felt, failed to do justice to Nicholson's story, and soured him on Hollywood. He was considering traveling around the country doing summer stock when he saw that photo of himself and Bruce Dern in that Toronto hotel room.

Fonda's post–*Easy Rider* career has been quirky and filled with flops that were both deserved and undeserved, and a few successes as well. "I've made some good movies and I've made a pile of bad ones," he has said.[257] Fonda is almost as famous for the parts he turned down as those he accepted, including leads in *Rosemary's Baby* (1968) and *Love Story* (1970). Early in his career he read for the role of John F. Kennedy in *PT 109* (1963), but lost out on the role when he insisted on doing it with a Kennedy-styled New England accent. Cliff Robertson eventually got the part, and played it accent-free.

In 2017, when Fonda was informed of his friend Jack Nicholson's rumored retirement, Fonda remarked, "Jack is retiring? . . . I don't want to retire. I feel like I'm about eight years old on most days."

When Dennis Hopper died in 2010, Peter Fonda had a hard time verbalizing the stormy relationship the two of them shared. He knew, of course, that both of them would always be linked together, always Billy and Captain America, always on that road. He finally released a statement, saying that "Dennis introduced me to the world of pop art and lost films. We rode the highways of America and changed the way movies were made in Hollywood. I was blessed by his friendship."[258]

That friendship was, almost from the start, a contentious one. Hopper had become convinced after the disastrous New Orleans shoot that

Fonda was trying to get him fired, and he wasn't entirely wrong. After that, their friendship was more a necessity and a convenience than an actual connection between the two. Hopper's temper and drug use during this period added to the distrust and animosity between them.

During *Easy Rider*'s post-production, Hopper tried to have Fonda's name removed from the writing credits. Fonda offered to take a "story by" credit instead, but when Hopper refused, Fonda, exasperated, then insisted that he get the full screenwriting credit which was specified in his contract. Dennis Hopper never forgot about this.

Jack Hunter points out (rather verbosely) in a book about Hopper, "[S]ignificantly, the rejection of a capitalist ideology, exposed by Hopper's character in *Easy Rider*, never seemed to have influenced his attitude towards the film's proceeds and dividends."[259] In 1970 Dennis Hopper sued Peter Fonda, for the first time (of many), over the percentage of the profits each was earning. Ironically, Hopper told the *New York Times*, "Peter and I have a wonderful relationship. Now that I'm suing him, he calls me more than he ever did before. That's the way it is, you see, when people get guilt feelings. He even offered to buy me a car. And neither of us has even mentioned the lawsuit. Peter and I will always be very close friends, no matter what. Like John Ford and Henry Fonda, like John Ford and Duke Wayne."[260]

But in 1992 Hopper sued his very close friend Peter Fonda again, this time over that screenwriting credit, and again Hopper insisted he receive a larger share of the film's profits. Out of court, the two actors' attorneys reached an agreement which kept Fonda's credit intact, but increased Hopper's share of the profits. Five years later Hopper again sued, this time claiming that the 1992 settlement had been breached. Again, the lawyers settled out of court, and this time the details were not disclosed.

In 1995, between lawsuits, Fonda mentioned in a documentary that Hopper was still fuming over this. "Dennis sent me a fax a couple months ago, and wanted me to sign a declaration that he and he alone had written the screenplay for *Easy Rider*. And I thought, this guy's out of his mind! Well, okay, I'll tell you what—I'll declare that the secretary and the secretary alone wrote the screenplay, because she applied fingers to typewriter keys . . . so in his mind he wrote it all by himself; he forgets the input that came from others. That's the way he is."[261]

Bill Hayward is quoted as agreeing with Fonda, more or less. "*Easy Rider* was written by three fucking loaded guys in a room. Somebody has the pencil and piece of paper, and that somebody wrote it all down. Dennis's position is that he had the piece of paper. I would tend to believe that Terry would more likely have had the piece of paper than Dennis would."[262]

Hopper would have none of this, however. "Okay, you can hear whatever you want, all right?" Hopper asserted. "This is it! I made that fucking movie! Period!"[263]

Regardless of all this animosity, in 1993 Hopper and Fonda, with country star Dwight Yoakam, opened a restaurant, Thunder Roadhouse, on the Sunset Strip in Hollywood. In spite of its biker vibe, the restaurant was actually named after a 1958 Robert Mitchum vehicle, or after a 1975 Bruce Springsteen song, depending on your point of reference. Like Fonda and Hopper's friendship, the restaurant proved to be highly combustible. Obvious bad karma led to its destruction by fire in 1997.

Hopper was married a total of five times, and was involved in a messy divorce with his last wife, Victoria Duffy, at the time of his death.

Hopper's professional life was just as troublesome as his personal one. Due to his drug and alcohol issues, he became largely unemployable as an actor, and certainly as a director, after *The Last Movie*. Eventually he moved to Taos, New Mexico, full-time, and concentrated on photography and art. In the early 1980s, however, he largely conquered his demons, and newly sober, and newly Republican, he returned to Hollywood and scored an Oscar nomination as an alcoholic coach in *Hoosiers* (1986). The same year he unforgettably appeared as a drug-addicted villain in David Lynch's terrifying *Blue Velvet* (1986). He continued to be in demand as a character actor, occasionally as a director, and as a living remnant of the counterculture and its demons, for the rest of his career.

By 2009, that long, strange career was winding down. Hopper had been diagnosed with pancreatic cancer, and was informed by his physicians that he had only a few months to live. His friends, and Hollywood at large, scrambled to award Hopper a star on Hollywood Boulevard's

Walk of Fame, although there was concern that the actor would not be well enough to attend the dedication. Hopper rallied, however, and although he looked gray and skeletal at the ceremony, held on March 25, 2010, he seemed to be in good spirits. Peter Fonda did not attend, but Jack Nicholson was there, and accompanied the frail Hopper to the podium. (Nicholson had received his own Walk of Fame star in 1996, and Fonda, in 2003.)

"You've shown me a world I would never have seen being a farm boy from Dodge City, Kansas," Hopper said, referring to his love/hate relationship with Hollywood, "learning things I would never have learned. I went under contract to Warner Bros. when I was eighteen years old, so my college, and everything I learned, I learned from Hollywood. And I've never been treated better by anyone. You shared your life with me and my talent and your talent. Everything I learned in life, I learned from you and the wonderful world that I traveled in and saw. Well, I got it all from you. So, this has been my home and my schooling, and I love all of you. Well, I just want to thank you, that's all I can do. This means so much to me, and thank you very much, everyone."[264]

Robert Walker remembers that "we hooked up again before he died; I went over to see him a number of times. His caretaker during those last months was the lady who was my mother's caretaker before she passed away. She took beautiful care of Dennis right up until the end."[265]

Dennis Hopper died two months after his Walk of Fame ceremony, on May 29. Walker, as well as both of his fellow easy riders, Fonda and Nicholson, this time attended the funeral. Although Fonda, as petty retribution for a thousand slights and lawsuits and percentage points and perceived injustices, was not invited inside the chapel. "I knew Dennis was dying, and I made many attempts to see Dennis, as did Bert Schneider. But he refused to see us. The funeral service was held in a chapel in Taos, New Mexico. I rented a private jet and flew in, but I was not allowed in the chapel. So, as much as I wanted to pay my respects, I was not allowed to be part of it," Fonda said regretfully in 2014.[266]

Jack Nicholson retained his composure during the ceremony, but when the casket was carried outside for burial, a gang of motorcyclists surrounding the chapel gunned their engines in respect, perhaps unintentionally evoking that photograph of a biker burial which had inspired *The Wild Angels* back in 1966. The roar of the choppers made Nicholson lose it. "When they set their engines off, that set me off too," Jack said.[267]

It has been fifty years since Peter Fonda and Dennis Hopper, Captain America and Billy, set off to look for America.

America is a very different place than it was fifty years ago. No goddamn doubt at all about that, as George Hanson might have put it. But then, what they were looking for, although they didn't know it at the time, is the same thing, and is at the same distant vanishing point it was at in 1969.

As Captain America aptly described it, they were looking to find their own thing. In their own time. Let's hope they find it.

Let's hope we all find it.

ENDNOTES

1. Feinberg, Scott, "TCM Film Fest: *Easy Rider* Icon Peter Fonda on Henry, Weed, Motorcycling and the MPAA," *The Hollywood Reporter*, March 31, 2015 (www.hollywoodreporter.com/race/tcm-film-fest-easy-rider-785315).

2. Hill, Lee. *A Grand Guy: The Art and Life of Terry Southern*. New York: Harper-Collins, 2001.

3. Fonda, Peter. *Don't Tell Dad: A Memoir*. New York: Hyperion, 1998.

4. Ibid.

5. Linderman, Lawrence. "*Playboy* Interview: Peter Fonda," *Playboy* (September 1970).

6. *Texas Monthly*. "The Checklist" (November 2015).

7. *Born to Be Wild: The Story of Easy Rider* (video, directed by Nick Freand Jones, UK: BBC2, 1995).

8. Ibid.

9. Lewis, Paul. "Easy Writer," *New Times Los Angeles*, March 4 1999.

10. *Born to Be Wild: The Story of Easy Rider* (video).

11. Ibid.

12. Biskind, Peter. *Easy Riders, Raging Bulls: How the Sex, Drugs and Rock 'n' Roll Generation Saved Hollywood*. New York: Simon & Schuster, 1998.

13. Fonda, *Don't Tell Dad: A Memoir*.

14. Corman, Roger, with Jim Jerome. *How I Made a Hundred Movies in Hollywood and Never Lost a Dime*. New York: Delta Press, 1990.

15. McGilligan, Patrick. *Jack's Life: A Biography of Jack Nicholson*. New York: W. W. Norton and Company, 1994.

16. Fonda, *Don't Tell Dad: A Memoir*.

17. *On the Trail of* Easy Rider*: 40 Years On . . . Still Searching for America* (video, directed by Simon Witter and Hannes Rossacher (UK: Studio-TV-Film GmbH, 2011).

18. *Born to Be Wild: The Story of Easy Rider* (video).

19. Ibid.

20. Biskind, *Easy Riders, Raging Bulls*.

21. Ibid.

22. Ibid.

23. Ibid.

24. *Easy Riders, Raging Bulls: How the Sex, Drugs and Rock 'n' Roll Generation Saved Hollywood* (video, directed by Kenneth Bowser, UK: BBC, 2003).

25. *Easy Rider* (1969) (DVD, The Criterion Collection, 2016), commentary track with Peter Fonda, Dennis Hopper, and Paul Lewis, recorded in 1995.

26. Interview, Don Cambern (February 13, 2019).

27. *History of the Chopper* (video, The Discovery Channel, 2010).

28. Fonda, *Don't Tell Dad: A Memoir*.

29. Carpenter, Susan. "Peter Fonda Goes His Way," *Los Angeles Times*, February 15, 2007.

30. *History of the Chopper* (video).

31. d'Orléans, Paul. *The Chopper: The Real Story*. New York: Gestalten, 2014.

32. Ibid.

33. *Born to Be Wild: The Story of Easy Rider* (video).

34. *Easy Rider: Shaking the Cage* (video, directed by Charles Kiselyak, Los Angeles: Columbia TriStar Home Video, 1999).

35. Carpenter, "Peter Fonda Goes His Way."

36. Interview, Mondo Porras (January 16, 2019).

37. *History of the Chopper* (video).

38. d'Orléans, *The Chopper: The Real Story*.

39. Warshow, Paul. "Easy Rider," *Sight and Sound* (Winter 1969–1970).

40. Biskind, *Easy Riders, Raging Bulls*.

41. "New York Social Diary: Your Link to Society" (Brooke Hayward's lunch with her family), February 14, 1981 (www.newyorksocialdiary.com/social-diary/2018/free-from-care).

42. Fleming, Charles. "Dennis Hopper Pal Michael Madsen Cries Foul on *Easy Rider* Bike Sale," *Los Angeles Times*, October 21, 2014.

43. Douglas, Illeana. *I Blame Dennis Hopper: And Other Stories from a Life Lived In and Out of the Movies*. New York: Flatiron Books, 2016.

44. *On the Trail of Easy Rider: 40 Years On* (video).

45. Ebert, Roger. *Roger Ebert's Video Companion* (1996 edition). Kansas City, MO: Andrews and McMeel, 1996.

46. *Easy Rider* (1969) (DVD, The Criterion Collection, 2016), commentary track with Dennis Hopper, recorded in 2009.

47. *On the Trail of Easy Rider: 40 Years On* (video).

48. Carson, L. M. "Kit." "*Easy Rider* Is a Very American Thing," *Evergreen* (November 1969).

49. *Born to Be Wild: The Story of Easy Rider* (video).

50. Interview, Robert Walker (February 26, 2019).

51. Ibid.

52. Winkler, Peter L. *Dennis Hopper: The Wild Ride of a Hollywood Rebel*. Fort Lee, NJ: Barricade Books, 2011.

53. Ibid.

54. Rodriguez, Elena. *Dennis Hopper: A Madness to His Method*. New York: St. Martin's Press, 1988.

55. McGilligan, *Jack's Life*.

56. Biskind, *Easy Riders, Raging Bulls*.

57. *Born to Be Wild: The Story of Easy Rider* (video).

58. *Easy Rider* (1969) (DVD, commentary track with Fonda, Hopper, and Lewis, 1995).

59. Interview, Robert Walker.

60. *Easy Rider* (1969) (DVD, commentary track with Fonda, Hopper, and Lewis, 1995).

61. Corman, Roger, with Jim Jerome. *How I Made a Hundred Movies in Hollywood and Never Lost a Dime*. New York: Delta Press, 1990.

62. *Easy Rider* (1969) (DVD, commentary track with Fonda, Hopper, and Lewis, 1995).

63. Zonkel, Philip. "Basil, Black and Fonda on *Easy Rider*," *Press Telegram*, October 3, 2003.

64. Winkler, *Dennis Hopper: The Wild Ride of a Hollywood Rebel.*

65. McGilligan, *Jack's Life.*

66. Winkler, *Dennis Hopper: The Wild Ride of a Hollywood Rebel.*

67. Interview, Donnie "Hair Bear" Derbes, conducted by Alan Dunn (February 2019).

68. *Easy Rider* (1969) (DVD, commentary track with Fonda, Hopper, and Lewis, 1995).

69. Linderman, "*Playboy* Interview: Peter Fonda."

70. McGilligan, *Jack's Life.*

71. Carson, "*Easy Rider* Is a Very American Thing."

72. Linderman, "*Playboy* Interview: Peter Fonda."

73. Zonkel, "Basil, Black and Fonda on *Easy Rider*."

74. Interview, Henry Jaglom, conducted by Alan Dunn (January 8, 2019).

75. *Easy Rider* (1969) (DVD, commentary track with Hopper, 2009).

76. *Easy Rider* (1969) (DVD, commentary track with Fonda, Hopper, and Lewis, 1995).

77. Krens, Thomas. *The Art of the Motorcycle* (Guggenheim Museum Publications). New York: Solomon R. Guggenheim Museum, 1998.

78. Mueller, Jim. "Heavy-Metal Thunder, Or Just an Imposter?" *Chicago Tribune*, January 10, 1999.

79. Linderman, "*Playboy* Interview: Peter Fonda."

80. Fonda, Peter. "Dennis the Menace," *Vanity Fair* (July 1987).

81. Carson, "*Easy Rider* Is a Very American Thing."

82. Winkler, *Dennis Hopper: The Wild Ride of a Hollywood Rebel.*

83. Rodriguez, *Dennis Hopper: A Madness to His Method.*

84. *Born to Be Wild: The Story of Easy Rider* (video).

85. *Easy Rider: Shaking the Cage* (video).

86. *Easy Rider* (1969) (DVD, commentary track with Hopper, 2009).

87. *On the Trail of* Easy Rider*: 40 Years On* (video).

88. *Born to Be Wild: The Story of Easy Rider* (video).

89. Ibid.

90. Peary, Danny. *Cult Movies 3*. New York: Fireside Books, Simon & Schuster, 1988.

91. *Born to Be Wild: The Story of Easy Rider* (video).

92. *Easy Rider: Shaking the Cage* (video).
93. Interview, Donn Cambern (February 13, 2019).
94. *Easy Rider: Shaking the Cage* (video).
95. Linderman, "*Playboy* Interview: Peter Fonda."
96. Interview, Donn Cambern.
97. Winkler, *Dennis Hopper: The Wild Ride of a Hollywood Rebel.*
98. Carson, "*Easy Rider* Is a Very American Thing."
99. *Easy Rider: Shaking the Cage* (video).
100. Interview, Donn Cambern.
101. *Born to Be Wild: The Story of Easy Rider* (video).
102. Interview, Donn Cambern.
103. Interview, Henry Jaglom.
104. Interview, Donn Cambern.
105. Interview, Henry Jaglom.
106. Ibid.
107. Interview, Donn Cambern.
108. Ibid.
109. Interview, Henry Jaglom.
110. Ibid.
111. Ibid.
112. *On the Trail of Easy Rider: 40 Years On* (video).
113. Rodriguez, *Dennis Hopper: A Madness to His Method.*
114. *Born to Be Wild: The Story of Easy Rider* (video).
115. Interview, Donn Cambern.
116. Fonda, *Don't Tell Dad: A Memoir.*
117. Winkler, *Dennis Hopper: The Wild Ride of a Hollywood Rebel.*
118. *Born to Be Wild: The Story of Easy Rider* (video).
119. *On the Trail of Easy Rider: 40 Years On* (video).
120. Interview, Donn Cambern.
121. *Steve Blauner* (video, directed by Kim Hendrickson, Los Angeles: The Criterion Collection, 2010).
122. Interview, Donn Cambern.
123. Biskind, *Easy Riders, Raging Bulls.*
124. Ibid.
125. *Steve Blauner* (video).
126. *Easy Riders, Raging Bulls* (video).
127. Crowther, Bosley. "Bonnie and Clyde," *New York Times*, April 14, 1967.
128. Canby, Vincent. "*Easy Rider*: A Statement on Film," *New York Times*, July 15, 1969.
129. Willis, Ellen. "See America First," *The New York Review of Books*, January 1, 1970.
130. *Village Voice.* "Easy Rider," July 3, 1969.
131. Schickel, Richard. "A Long Tragic Story of the Road," *Life*, July 11, 1969.
132. Kael, Pauline. *For Keeps: 30 Years at the Movies.* New York: Plume, 1996.
133. Kaufman, Stanley. "Stanley Kaufman on Film," *The New Republic*, August 2, 1969.

134. Brackman, Jacob. *"Easy Rider," Esquire* (September 1969).

135. Hampton, Claude C. "Movies that Play for Keeps," *Film Comment* (Fall 1970).

136. Milne, Tom. *"Easy Rider," Sight and Sound* (August 1969).

137. Farber, Manny. *"Easy Rider," Artforum* (October 1969).

138. Haycock, Joel, *"Easy Rider* at the Charles Street Cinemas, with Long Lines," *Harvard Crimson*, August 12, 1969.

139. Ibid.

140. Ebert, Roger. *"Easy Rider," Chicago Sun-Times*, September 28, 1969.

141. Champlin, Charles. "Low Cost, High Importance Biker Film," *Los Angeles Times*, August 10, 1969.

142. Moskowitz, Gene. *"Easy Rider," Daily Variety*, May 14, 1969.

143. Mahoney, John. *"Easy Rider," The Hollywood Reporter*, June 26, 1969.

144. Everett, Todd. "Hopper, Fonda Film Exceptionally Done," *Hollywood Citizen News*, August 12, 1969.

145. Ibid.

146. Gertner, Richard. *"Easy Rider," Motion Picture Herald*, July 16, 1969.

147. Ibid.

148. Blevins, Winfred. "Cruisin' with Easy Rider," *Los Angeles Harold Examiner*, August 10, 1969.

149. Ibid.

150. Polk, Harriet R. *"Easy Rider," Film Quarterly* (Fall 1969).

151. Mayer, James A. *"Easy Rider* Will Turn Off Any Over-30 Movie Viewer," *Miami Herald*, October, 3, 1969.

152. Flynn, Charles, "Fashionably Bleak, *Easy Rider, The Rain People*, and *Medium Cool,"* Focus* (October 1969).

153. Ibid.

154. Driscoll, O'Connel. *"Easy Rider* Revisited," Show (June 1970).

155. Naughton, James M. "Agnew Assails Songs and Films that Promote a 'Drug Culture,'" *New York Times*, September 15, 1970.

156. Ibid.

157. Farber, Stephen. "End of the Road," *Film Quarterly* (Winter 1969–1970).

158. Collins, Mark. "Peter Fonda Knew Easy Rider Was Unique," *The Daily Camera*, February 9, 2013.

159. Flatley, Guy. "Henry Fonda Takes Aim at . . . ," *New York Times*, October 18, 1970.

160. Flatley, Guy. D-e-n-n-i-s. H-o-p-p-e-r!" *New York Times*, October 18, 1970.

161. Linderman, *"Playboy* Interview: Peter Fonda."

162. Biskind, *Easy Riders, Raging Bulls.*

163. Ibid.

164. Karen, Howard. "Young Americans," *Premiere* (Winter 1999).

165. Winkler, *Dennis Hopper: The Wild Ride of a Hollywood Rebel.*

166. Ibid.

167. Biskind, Peter. "Ballad of Easy Rider," *Premiere* (July 1997).

168. Ebert, Roger. "Dennis Hopper: In Memory," *Chicago Sun-Times*, May 29, 2010.

169. Winkler, *Dennis Hopper: The Wild Ride of a Hollywood Rebel.*

170. *American Film.* "Ghost Riders in the Sky" (June 1983).

171. *Rolling Stone.* "An *Easy Rider* Sequel Planned," October 14, 1982.

172. Winkler, *Dennis Hopper: The Wild Ride of a Hollywood Rebel.*

173. Maltin, Leonard. *Leonard Maltin's 2015 Movie Guide.* New York: Plume/Penguin, 2015.

174. "Ask an Actor: Peter Fonda/BFI," part one, British Film Institute, published July 14, 2014, YouTube (www.youtube.com/watch?v=f7g_vMAYvWI&t=119s).

175. Ibid.

176. Gillis, J. F. X. "Easy Rider: Right-Wing Classic?" *New York Times,* June 8, 2010.

177. Mavis, Paul. Essay on *Easy Rider: The Ride Back,* DVD Talk (www.dvdtalk.com/reviews/61663/easy-rider-the-ride-back/).

178. Rabin, Nathan. Essay on *Easy Rider: The Ride Back,* The Dissolve.com (https://thedissolve.com/features/you-might-also-like/486-yes-theres-an-easy-rider-sequel-and-yes-its-awful/).

179. *Easy Rider: The Ride Back* official website (www.easyridertherideback.com/).

180. *On the Trail of* Easy Rider*: 40 Years On* (video).

181. Ibid.

182. Dowd, Maureen. "Bush Boasts of Turnaround from *Easy Rider* Society," *New York Times,* October 7, 1988.

183. Ebert, *Roger Ebert's Video Companion* (1996 edition).

184. Ibid.

185. Interview, Donnie "Hair Bear" Derbes.

186. Zonkel, "Basil, Black and Fonda on *Easy Rider.*"

187. Nichols, Dave. *One Percenter: The Legend of the Outlaw Biker.* Minneapolis, MN: Motorbooks, 2010.

188. Winkler, *Dennis Hopper: The Wild Ride of a Hollywood Rebel.*

189. Macaulay, Sean. "Nostalgia Takes a Queasy Ride," *London Times,* September 22, 1999.

190. Uhlich, Keith. "Easy Rider," *Time Out New York,* January 1, 2010.

191. Neibaur, James L. *The Essential Jack Nicholson.* Lanham, MD: Rowman & Littlefield, 2017.

192. Bayer, William. *Breaking Through, Selling Out, Dropping Dead and Other Notes on Filmmaking.* New York: Proscenium Publications, 1989.

193. Interview, Robert Walker.

194. Fonda, *Don't Tell Dad: A Memoir.*

195. Nichols, Dave. *One Percenter: The Legend of the Outlaw Biker.*

196. Ibid.

197. Interview, Mondo Porras.

198. "Peter Fonda and the Captain America Bike" (video), 2009 (www.youtube.com/watch?v=EbKSXkvV9FE&feature=youtu.be).

199. Carnell, Sarah, "Graham Gamble," *Motorcycle Times* (February 2009).

200. Interview, Dave Nichols (January 15, 2019).

201. Interview, Blue Miller, conducted by Alan Dunn (February 2019).

202. Interview, Daryl "Caveman" Nelson, conducted by Alan Dunn (February 2019).

203. Interview, Randy Beckstrand, conducted by Alan Dunn (February 2019).

204. Interview, Tom Elliot, conducted by Alan Dunn (February 2019).

205. Interview, Jim Griffin, conducted by Alan Dunn (February, 2019).

206. Interview, Skip Wiatrolik (February 27, 2019).

207. Ibid.

208. *On the Trail of* Easy Rider*: 40 Years On* (video).

209. Interview, George Christie, conducted by Alan Dunn (February 18, 2019).

210. Barth, Jack, and Trey Ellis. "*Easy Rider* Revisited," *Premiere* (May 1989).

211. Ibid.

212. Ibid.

213. Ibid.

214. Ibid.

215. Ibid.

216. Douglas, *I Blame Dennis Hopper.*

217. Ibid.

218. Ibid.

219. "Illeana Douglas Top 10" (www.criterion.com/current/top-10-lists/296-illeana
-douglas-s-top-10).

220. Linderman, "*Playboy* Interview: Peter Fonda."

221. Carson, "*Easy Rider* Is a Very American Thing."

222. Biskind, *Easy Riders, Raging Bulls.*

223. Interview, Henry Jaglom.

224. Interview, Donn Cambern.

225. Biskind, *Easy Riders, Raging Bulls.*

226. *Easy Riders, Raging Bulls* (video).

227. Interview, Donn Cambern.

228. *Easy Riders, Raging Bulls* (video).

229. Davis, Peter. "Remembering Bert Schneider," *Huffington Post*, December 28, 2011.

230. *Easy Riders, Raging Bulls* (video).

231. Ibid.

232. Ibid.

233. Interview, David McGiffert (February 2, 2019).

234. "Bill Hayward Dies at 66." *Daily Variety*, March 21, 2008.

235. Interview, David McGiffert.

236. Ibid.

237. Interview, Mondo Porras.

238. Mueller, "Heavy-Metal Thunder, Or Just an Imposter?"

239. *New York Post.* "*Easy Rider* Bike Going to Auction," September 17, 2014.

240. Miller, Stuart. "The Battle Over Captain America, the Chopper from *Easy Rider*,"
Maxim, April 10, 2015.

241. Mueller, "Heavy-Metal Thunder, Or Just an Imposter?"

242. Miller, "The Battle Over Captain America."

243. *On the Trail of* Easy Rider*: 40 Years On* (video).

244. Flatley, "Henry Fonda Takes Aim at . . ."

245. Feinberg, "TCM Film Fest: *Easy Rider* Icon Peter Fonda."

246. Ibid.

247. *Time.* "Cinema: John Wayne as the Last Hero," August 8, 1969.

248. *On the Trail of* Easy Rider*: 40 Years On* (video).

249. *Easy Rider: Shaking the Cage* (video).

250. Thomas, Bryan. "Over My Head: Toni Basil's 1984 Video Arrived in What Was Then the Third Decade of Her Career," Nightflight, July 11, 2017 (http://nightflight .com/over-my-head-toni-basils-1984-video/).

251. Golden, Mike. "Terry Southern: Writing to His Own Beat," *Creative Screenwriting,* January 12, 2016.

252. Hill, Lee. *A Grand Guy: The Art and Life of Terry Southern.* New York: Harper-Collins, 2001.

253. Ibid.

254. Katz, Ephraim. *The Film Encyclopedia.* New York: HarperCollins, 1994.

255. Carpenter, "Peter Fonda Goes His Way."

256. Ibid.

257. Feinberg, "TCM Film Fest: *Easy Rider* Icon Peter Fonda."

258. Winkler, *Dennis Hopper: The Wild Ride of a Hollywood Rebel.*

259. Hunter, Jack (ed.). Essay by Mikita Brottman. *Dennis Hopper Movie Top Ten.* UK: Creation Books International, 1999.

260. Flatley, "D-e-n-n-i-s. H-o-p-p-e-r!" *New York Times,* October 18, 1970.

261. *Born to Be Wild: The Story of Easy Rider* (video).

262. Winkler, *Dennis Hopper: The Wild Ride of a Hollywood Rebel.*

263. *Born to Be Wild: The Story of Easy Rider* (video).

264. Winkler, *Dennis Hopper: The Wild Ride of a Hollywood Rebel.*

265. Interview, Robert Walker.

266. Aftab, Kaleem. "Dennis Hopper: Peter Fonda on His *Easy Rider* Co-Star," *Independent Minds,* July 15, 2014.

267. Winkler, *Dennis Hopper: The Wild Ride of a Hollywood Rebel.*

Bibliography

Books

Barth, Jack. *Roadside Hollywood*. Chicago: Contemporary Books, 1991.

Bayer, William. *Breaking Through, Selling Out, Dropping Dead and Other Notes on Film-making*. New York: Proscenium Publications, 1989.

Biskind, Peter. *Easy Riders, Raging Bulls: How the Sex, Drugs and Rock 'n' Roll Generation Saved Hollywood*. New York: Simon & Schuster, 1998.

Corman, Roger, with Jim Jerome. *How I Made a Hundred Movies in Hollywood and Never Lost a Dime*. New York: Delta Press, 1990.

Dawson, Nick (ed.). *Dennis Hopper Interviews*. Jackson: University Press of Mississippi, 2012.

d'Orléans, Paul. *The Chopper: The Real Story*. New York: Gestalten, 2014.

Douglas, Illeana. *I Blame Dennis Hopper: And Other Stories from a Life Lived In and Out of the Movies*. New York: Flatiron Books, 2016.

Ebert, Roger. *Roger Ebert's Video Companion* (1996 edition). Kansas City, MO: Andrews and McMeel, 1996.

Folsom, Scott. *Hopper*. New York: HarperCollins, 2013.

Fonda, Peter. *Don't Tell Dad: A Memoir*. New York: Hyperion, 1998.

Hayward, Brooke. *Haywire.* New York: Alfred A. Knopf, 1977.

Hill, Lee. *A Grand Guy: The Art and Life of Terry Southern*. New York: HarperCollins, 2001.

Hunter, Jack (ed.). Essay by Mikita Brottman. *Dennis Hopper Movie Top Ten*. UK: Creation Books International, 1999.

Kael, Pauline. *For Keeps: 30 Years at the Movies*. New York: Plume, 1996.

Katz, Ephraim. *The Film Encyclopedia*. New York: HarperCollins, 1994.

Krens, Thomas. *The Art of the Motorcycle* (Guggenheim Museum Publications). New York: Solomon R. Guggenheim Museum, 1998.

Maltin, Leonard. *Leonard Maltin's 2015 Movie Guide*. New York: Plume/Penguin, 2015.

McGilligan, Patrick. *Jack's Life: A Biography of Jack Nicholson*. New York: W. W. Norton and Company, 1994.

Neibaur, James L. *The Essential Jack Nicholson*. Lanham, MD: Rowman & Littlefield, 2017.

Nichols, Dave. *One Percenter: The Legend of the Outlaw Biker*. Minneapolis, MN: Motor-books, 2010.

Osgerby, Bill. *Biker: Truth and Myth*. Guilford, CT: The Lyons Press, 2005.

Peary, Danny. *Cult Movies 3*. New York: Fireside Books, Simon & Schuster, 1988.

Rodriguez, Elena. *Dennis Hopper: A Madness to His Method*. New York: St. Martin's Press, 1988.

Thompson, Hunter S. *Hell's Angels: A Strange and Terrible Saga*. New York: Ballantine Books, 1967.

Wakeman, John. *World Film Directors, Volume 2*. Hackensack, NJ: The H. W. Wilson Company, 1988.

Winkler, Peter L. *Dennis Hopper: The Wild Ride of a Hollywood Rebel*. Fort Lee, NJ: Barricade Books, 2011.

PERIODICALS

Aftab, Kaleem. "Dennis Hopper: Peter Fonda on His *Easy Rider* Co-Star," *Independent Minds*, July 15, 2014.

American Film. "Ghost Riders in the Sky" (June 1983).

Barth, Jack, and Trey Ellis. "*Easy Rider* Revisited," *Premiere* (May 1989).

Biskind, Peter. "Ballad of Easy Rider," *Premiere* (July 1997).

Blevins, Winfred. "Cruisin' with *Easy Rider*," *Los Angeles Herald Examiner*, August 10, 1969.

Brackman, Jacob. "*Easy Rider*," *Esquire* (September 1969).

Canby, Vincent. "*Easy Rider*: A Statement on Film," *New York Times*, July 15, 1969.

Carnell, Sarah. "Graham Gamble," *Motorcycle Times* (February 2009).

Carpenter, Susan. "Peter Fonda Goes His Way," *Los Angeles Times*, February 15, 2007.

Carson, L. M. "Kit." "*Easy Rider* Is a Very American Thing," *Evergreen* (November 1969).

Champlin, Charles. "Low Cost, High Importance Biker Film," *Los Angeles Times*, August 10, 1969.

Collins, Mark. "Peter Fonda Knew *Easy Rider* Was Unique," *The Daily Camera*, February 9, 2013.

Crowther, Bosley. "Bonnie and Clyde," *New York Times*, April 14, 1967.

Dagen, Carmel. "Steve Blauner, Who Helped Bring *Easy Rider*, *Five Easy Pieces* to Screen, Dies at 81," *Daily Variety*, June 17, 2015.

Daily Variety. "Bill Hayward Dies at 66," March 21, 2008.

Davis, Peter. "Remembering Bert Schneider," *Huffington Post*, December 28, 2011.

Dowd, Maureen. "Bush Boasts of Turnaround from *Easy Rider* Society," *New York Times*, October 7, 1988.

Driscoll, O'Connel. "*Easy Rider* Revisited," *Show* (June 1970).

Ebert, Roger. "*Easy Rider*," *Chicago Sun-Times*, September 28, 1969.

———. "Dennis Hopper: In Memory," *Chicago-Sun Times*, May 29, 2010.

Everett, Todd. "Hopper, Fonda Film Exceptionally Done," *Hollywood Citizen News*, August 12, 1969.

Farber, Manny. "*Easy Rider*," *Artforum* (October 1969).

Farber, Stephen. "End of the Road," *Film Quarterly* (Winter 1969–1970).

Flatley, Guy. "Henry Fonda Takes Aim at . . . ," *New York Times*, October 17, 1970.

————. "D-e-n-n-i-s. H-o-p-p-e-r!" *New York Times*, October 18, 1970.

Fleming, Charles. "Dennis Hopper Pal Michael Madsen Cries Foul on *Easy Rider* Bike Sale," *Los Angeles Times*, October 21, 2014.

————. "*Easy Rider* Bike Designer Cliff Vaughs, 79, Lived Many Lives: Photographer, Filmmaker, Boat Captain," *Los Angeles Times*, July 8, 2016.

Flynn, Charles. "Fashionably Bleak, *Easy Rider*, *The Rain People*, and *Medium Cool*," *Focus* (October 1969).

Fonda, Peter. "Dennis the Menace," *Vanity Fair* (July 1987).

Frank, Aaron. "Captain America Motorcycle—Up to Speed," *Motorcyclist*, August 4, 2009.

Gertner, Richard. "*Easy Rider*," *Motion Picture Herald*, July 16, 1969.

Gillis, J. F. X. "*Easy Rider*: Right-Wing Classic?" *New York Times*, June 8, 2010.

Golden, Mike. "Terry Southern: Writing to His Own Beat," *Creative Screenwriting*, January 12, 2016.

Hampton, Claude C. "Movies that Play for Keeps," *Film Comment* (Fall 1970).

Harris, Dana. "*New Rider* a 'Miracle' Pic," *Daily Variety*, May 15, 2000.

Haycock, Joel. "*Easy Rider* at the Charles Street Cinemas, with Long Lines," *Harvard Crimson*, August 12, 1969.

Karen, Howard. "Young Americans," *Premiere* (Winter 1999).

Kaufman, Stanley. "Stanley Kaufman on Film," *The New Republic*, August 2, 1969.

King, Thomas R. "Hey, Man, See You in Court: *Easy Rider* Gets a New Epilogue," *Wall Street Journal*, February 9, 1996.

Lewis, Paul. "Easy Writer," *New Times Los Angeles*, March 4, 1999.

Linderman, Lawrence. "*Playboy* Interview: Peter Fonda," *Playboy* (September 1970).

Macaulay, Sean. "Nostalgia Takes a Queasy Ride," *London Times*, September 22, 1999.

Mahoney, John. "*Easy Rider*," *The Hollywood Reporter*, June 26, 1969.

Mayer, James A. "*Easy Rider* Will Turn Off Any Over-30 Movie Viewer," *Miami Herald*, October 3, 1969.

McGilligan, Patrick. "The Ballad of *Easy Rider*," *Los Angeles Magazine* (March 1994).

Miller, Stuart. "The Battle Over Captain America, the Chopper from *Easy Rider*," *Maxim*, April 10, 2015.

Milne, Tom. "*Easy Rider*," *Sight and Sound* (August 1969).

Moerk, Christian. "*Easy Rider* Rides Again. Or Does It?" *New York Times*, March 19, 2006.

Moskowitz, Gene. "*Easy Rider*," *Daily Variety*, May 14, 1969.

Mueller, Jim. "Heavy-Metal Thunder, Or Just an Imposter?" *Chicago Tribune*, January 10, 1999.

Naughton, James M. "Agnew Assails Songs and Films that Promote a 'Drug Culture,'" *New York Times*, September 15, 1970.

New York Post. "*Easy Rider* Bike Going to Auction," September 17, 2014.

Polk, Harriet R. "*Easy Rider*," *Film Quarterly* (Fall 1969).

Rolling Stone. "An *Easy Rider* Sequel Planned," October 14, 1982.

Schickel, Richard. "A Long Tragic Story of the Road," *Life*, July 11, 1969.

Texas Monthly. "The Checklist" (November 2015).

Time. "Cinema: John Wayne as the Last Hero," August 8, 1969.

Uhlich, Keith. *"Easy Rider," Time Out New York,* January 1, 2010.

Village Voice. "Easy Rider," July 3, 1969.

Warshow, Paul. *"Easy Rider," Sight and Sound* (Winter 1969–1970).

Willis, Ellen. "See America First," *The New York Review of Books,* January 1, 1970.

Zonkel, Philip. "Basil, Black and Fonda on *Easy Rider,*" *Press Telegram,* October 3, 2003.

WEBSITES

"Ask an Actor: Peter Fonda/BFI." British Film Institute, published July 14, 2014, YouTube (www.youtube.com/watch?v=f7g_vMAYvWI&t=119s and www.youtube .com/watch?time_continue=16&v=f7g_vMAYvWI).

Christie, George. Blog (www.georgechristie.com/about.html).

Denver's Choppers (https://denverschoppers.com/).

Dunn, Alan. "Mr. Zip 66: Road Blogging and Life on a Harley-Davidson" (www .mrzip66.com/).

EagleRider *Easy Rider* Motorcycle Tour (www.eaglerider.com/guided-motorcycle -tours/eagleriders-easy-rider-movie-tour-inspired-by-the-major-motion-picture -easy-rider).

Easy Rider: The Ride Back (www.easyridertherideback.com/index.html).

Easyriders Magazine (www.magazine-agent.com-sub.info/Easyriders/Welcome).

Feinberg, Scott. Podcast interview with Peter Fonda, "TCM Film Fest: *Easy Rider* Icon Peter Fonda on Henry, Weed, Motorcycling and the MPAA," *The Hollywood Reporter,* March 31, 2015 (www.hollywoodreporter.com/race/tcm-film-fest-easy -rider-785315).

Fonda, Peter. "Peter Fonda and the Captain America Bike," 2009, YouTube (www .youtube.com/watch?v=EbKSXkvV9FE&feature=youtu.be).

"Illeana Douglas Top 10," The Criterion Collection (www.criterion.com/current/top -10-lists/296-illeana-douglas-s-top-10).

Mavis, Paul. Essay on *Easy Rider: The Ride Back,* DVD Talk (www.dvdtalk.com/ reviews/61663/easy-rider-the-ride-back/).

"New York Social Diary: Your Link to Society" (Brooke Hayward's lunch with her family), February 14, 1981 (www.newyorksocialdiary.com/social-diary/2018/ free-from-care).

Rabin, Nathan. Essay on *Easy Rider: The Ride Back,* The Dissolve.com (https://thedissolve .com/features/you-might-also-like/486-yes-theres-an-easy-rider-sequel-and-yes -its-awful/).

Sugar Bear Choppers (www.sugarbearchoppers.com/).

Thomas, Bryan. "Over My Head: Toni Basil's 1984 Video Arrived in What Was Then the Third Decade of Her Career," Nightflight, July 11, 2017 (http://nightflight .com/over-my-head-toni-basils-1984-video/).

VIDEOS

Along for the Ride (The Orchard, 2017).

America Lost and Found: The BBS Story (The Criterion Collection, 2010).

Born to Be Wild: The Story of Easy Rider (directed by Nick Freand Jones, UK: BBC2, 1995).

Easy Rider (1969) (The Criterion Collection, 2016). Contains two audio commentaries, one with Dennis Hopper (2009), the other with Hopper, Peter Fonda, and production manager Paul Lewis (1995); footage of Hopper and Fonda at the 1969 Cannes Film Festival; the film's trailers; and the documentaries *Born to be Wild* (1995), *Easy Rider: Shaking the Cage* (1999), and *Steve Blauner* (2010).

Easy Rider: Shaking the Cage (directed by Charles Kiselyak, Los Angeles: Columbia TriStar Home Video, 1999).

Easy Rider: The Ride Back (Kino Lorber, 2013).

Easy Riders, Raging Bulls: How the Sex, Drugs and Rock 'n' Roll Generation Saved Hollywood (directed by Kenneth Bowser, UK: BBC, 2003).

History of the Chopper (The Discovery Channel, 2010).

On the Trail of Easy Rider*: 40 Years On . . . Still Searching for America* (directed by Simon Witter and Hannes Rossacher, UK: Studio-TV-Film GmbH, 2011).

Steve Blauner (directed by Kim Hendrickson, Los Angeles: The Criterion Collection, 2010).

Then Came Bronson (1969) (Warner Home Video, 2010).

INTERVIEWS

Beckstrand, Randy (February 2019, conducted by Alan Dunn).

Cambern, Donn (February 13, 2019).

Christie, George (February 18, 2019, conducted by Alan Dunn).

Derbes, Donnie "Hair Bear" (February 2019, conducted by Alan Dunn).

Elliot, Tom (February 2019, conducted by Alan Dunn).

Griffin, Jim (February 2019, conducted by Alan Dunn).

Jaglom, Henry (January 8, 2019).

King, Joyce (March 10, 2019, conducted by Joan Ksbosius).

McGiffert, David (February 2, 2019).

Miller, Blue (February 2019, conducted by Alan Dunn).

Nelson, Daryl "Caveman" (February 2019, conducted by Alan Dunn).

Nichols, Dave (January 15, 2019).

Porras, Mondo (January 16, 2019).

Walker, Robert (February 26, 2019).

Wiatrolik, Skip (February 27, 2019).

Index